UNFIN-

Thank you to the Author of my story.
For creating something beautiful
From someone whose seen and done so much ugliness.
Thank you for allowing me to borrow this talent and use it to
show people that you truly do love the ratchet.
I pray that I use my gifts and platform to honor you so
when it's all given back at the end of I can be sure to hear
your loving voice say, "Well done".

Table of Contents

......

Acknowledgements

You know what? I find this section very difficult to fill. Not because I can't think of anyone who I can count worthy enough to be acknowledged; that'd be madly dishonoring. More so because I cannot honestly think of one person, place, thing, force, circumstance, situation, achievement, failure, heartbreak, smile, tear, sunrise, sunset, full moon, depression season, nor everyday reminder of hope that doesn't deserve acknowledgement to this work that you have in your hands right now. I deserve very little thanks; for I am only the vessel in which all these things pour themselves into. All I did was be.

But I will thank those that first come to my mind and heart. I will start off by being that cliché individual by thanking my family. Thank you, mom. Thank you, dad. For letting me be me, even when it brought great concern to you two. Thank you for always allowing me to test the waters only to come to the realization that I can't swim...and then fishing me out! Through your apprehensive trust to my reckless decisions, risky moves in life, you exemplified faith in God and His directing of my footsteps. Even when journeys brought me to places of deep scars and bruises; both inflicted by others and myself, I learned great and valuable wisdom that I treasure for all days of my life. This would never happen if you two didn't let me fly with the premature, unlearned wings. I owe everything and more to you two. I also thank my younger brother and sister for the laughs, the jokes, the arguing, the fighting, the borrowing of clothes that existed between my brother and I, and the random Facebook video shares that still go on between my sister and I. Thank you too, for putting up with me having the responsibility of being the older sibling. Regardless of our awkward interactions, I want you two to know that I love you both, and that I hope that you two seeing my life transform over the years reminds you that God is always using every experience you two go through to remind you how loved and valued you are by Him.

And here's to everyone else! Thank you to my best friend, brother, mentor, and pastor, Anthony Flanigan. I don't think I could ever be thankful enough for part time jobs just to get me through college! Who ever knew that meeting in a shoe store while I was working would lead up to this moment. Thank you for believing in me, for being a friend who always pushed me to be better than I believed myself to be. Thank you for showing me that many things about myself that I didn't know existed, and the great things outside myself that I still had yet to humbly learn. Thank you for spending many years of sacrificed time, money, patience, and resources all because you believed in God's plan for my life. I wish people could see how much you and your wife April, and your children Titus and Selah, and your church have done for me. Thank you for being my biggest fan, and for being there for me. I'd also like to thank my other brother Jeremiah. I thank you for being the exact opposite of me; energetic, in your face with positivity, hyperactive, and madly extrovert; we bring great balance to each other's lives. I thank you for teaching me how to show up and be vulnerable. If I didn't have you in my life, life would kind of suck! I mean, you showed me how to rap...a white guy taught a brown individual how to rap! Being able to know you from elementary school till now, and see your grow in your faith has been the most inspiring and amazing privilege ever. I love you man. Thank you, Dan Fenessy, for being risky enough to ask me to perform at your open mic years ago. You are kind of the reason this book is here! Big thanks to the O.G. of Quad City Poetry, Chris Britton! If I had never come to your poetry slam years ago, I wouldn't have been caught by Dan, writing poetry at Coolbeanz, which led to spitting at his open mic! Look at all the connections! Thank you Gerald Aloran, who I by 'chance' happened to pull up a seat next to at a conference in Madison Wisconsin, with an audience of about two thousand people, only to find out we lived in the same area! You expanded my mind and how to look at the world, how to view my faith and how to be a greater witness through all avenues I choose to impact the world by. You are amazing! Thank you Terrell Boyd for being at that open mic in Moline at the Ford's church coincidentally the same time I was. You've pushed me hard in taking on the arts full time, and to just being more honest with myself in personal endeavors. It has hurt, it has pissed me off sometimes, it has made me scared for my life, but this rollercoaster ride has been one helluva ride. Thank you for making me take risks. Thank you to Kermit Thomas, who was the reason that I have fans in Atlanta, Georgia and North Carolina! Thank you for believing in my art enough to take me on tour outside the state, and to continually encourage me. Thank you Ron AKA Drew Talent for always being real and edgy, and Joe Tingle for being more than an individual who has supported me with video and photo productions when I needed it; but for being the behind the scenes guy who was always pushing me to being smarter, wiser, and faithful with how I spend my life. Man, the arts community of the Quad Cities; thank you Ryan Collins of Midwest Writing Center for seeing so much worth in worthless me! Thank you Laura Winton AKA Fluffy Singler for Karawane: And the Temporary Death of Bruitist. Thank you Sean Whitney for Garage3; the DOPEST open mic in the Quad Cities! And extended thanks to Dylan and Tia Parker for allowing their garage to be the location of this madness! Thank you Beej and Nu Gruv Family, y'all have taught me so much! Oh! And thanks to-

These Poems...

Are not an art gallery of flawless work. These poems are an extension of my heart, my being, and my passion. A few weeks ago, I was hanging out with my friend and pastor Jason, and he brought up this quote from an artist, which I cannot remember word for word... But the gist of the quote was this: as a creative being, whether 'hobbyist' or professional, we focus too much on quality and not enough on quantity. We don't like to create unless we know it will be good enough, and so we forsake the blessing of just creating just to create. The soul of the artist is to not make perfection, but to make a whole bunch of imperfection. I say this in hopes that it drops boulders from your shoulders, giving you the freedom to accept yourself, accept your creative abilities as they are now, and never worry about the next man. Your art is valuable because it is from you. There is only one you. So, create! Believe that your work will always be good, because God is good.

My Dream

"Art and life really are the same, and both can only be about a spiritual journey, a path towards a re-union with a supreme creator, with god, with the divine; and this is true no matter how unlikely, how strange, how unorthodox, one's particular life path might appear to one's self or others at any given moment."

Genesis Breyer P-Orridge

"Would you like to read your poem this Saturday at the coffee shop I work at? We are looking to do new stuff for our open mic!" This is the invitation I was met with on May 12, 2014, by a random guy who would end up being my closest friend, brother, and the one who inadvertently pushed me out of my comfort zone down a path of life that I would never have foreseen. I owe this book to that friend... Dan. Who ran into me at the local coffee shop at home in Rock Island called "Coolbeanz", and interrupted my introverted time as I sat in the back-corner jotting down all these words, ideas, and feelings that were hitting me all at once due to one curious summer camp participant's question to me: "What did you want to be when you grew up?" Any other day I would have just wrote down in plain language my ponderings in one of those 100 sheets, 200 pages black and white covered composition notebooks (from my 2010 freshmen year of college up until then, I had about six of those notebooks filled... and they are in my parents' basement to this day collecting dust). I had caught the poetry bug after attending my first poetry slam March 29th of that year. It changed my perception of poetry, and dropped a match upon the tinder of my soul. I had already been a writer before that, since I was twelve to be exact, but like anyone else; writing poems in my journal whenever I was feeling some type of unexplainable way, but nothing impressive or written for the sake of the public. I even majored in English/writing my freshmen year of college at Iowa Central Community College in hopes of being a short story writer but switched majors out of external and internal pressures that told me to pursue a "real" major since being an author seemed like a poor degree when it came to making money in the "real" world. I say all this to say that I had always had a love and passion for poetry and dreamed to be a writer who could share and articulate his life experiences (even as a junior high student...) to inspire, touch, and encourage others. That dream though, had been suffocated like a wildfire doused by expectations, left-brained logic, safety and a lack of faith. This invitation from Dan was more than an open mic to me, and more than just sharing poetry. It was the opportunity of redemption; an opportunity to return back to that twelve-year-old me, kneel down and touch his shoulder and say, "your dream was accomplished; be joyful." I would like to say all this was going through my mind at that time, but to be honest when I was asked to read my poem, I had no idea what I was getting myself into. I didn't mind being in front of people and speaking, since interning at a church in Leclaire Iowa that gave me the responsibilities of preaching occasionally and leading a young adult bible study group prepped me for that. But doing poetry? Vulnerable poetry? Mind you this was my first poem written in some years. Nonetheless, I breathed in and prepped myself. From Monday to Wednesday I spent my time writing this poem, then from Thursday to Saturday I am mashing these words into my memory box, since I at least wanted my first time to "look" professional, and not relying on scratchy paper in front of me. Then come Saturday night at what used to be known as the East Village Cafe in Davenport Iowa. It was a cafe/bar that was once a horseshoe house (for the lack of better term) that sat on the end of all the bars on this small strip called The East Village. It was a small venue that attracted a lot of older folks who wanted a good time out on the weekends without all the elements of loud music and loud people. It was relaxed and welcoming. There were about eight people total here at this event not expecting poetry. My mom, aunt, and my two friends Santiago and Jeremiah came out for what could be a great triumph or a great failure. I breathed in, breathed out, meditated on that dream I wanted to cross off this bucket list, stared out at the crowd, and went in like I had been a veteran at this. That venue, that poetry, that passion, that dream, would tear the veil from in front of me, and reveal to me a new, untraveled, patiently waiting path that would change my life indefinitely. This story is still-

Make Your Own Table

"A pessimist sees the difficulty in every opportunity; an optimist sees the opportunity in every difficulty."

Winston S. Churchill

Remember that old quote, "give someone an inch and they'll go a mile?" Well, in this part of the story I was that someone. After my first open mic, that fire to write was rekindled and by the looks of it had no desire to go out anytime soon. I started learning the craft a little from a few homies in the area who got me interested in the arts in the first place; my good friend Jeremiah who had been emceeing for some years; Marcos who would stay up with me after long hours of working just to talk poetry and write some new stuff; Chris who is literally (even to this day, whatever this day entails) the OG of this poetry culture that was starting to thrive in the Quad City area; and my very good friend, brother, and mentor Anthony Flanigan who saw my talent before anyone else and heavily invested in that.. even when it came to criticisms that pissed me off for a few days. But anyway, Anthony and I had been coming back on a weekly basis to East Village Cafe to share poetry with the crowd along with some comedians who weren't that fond of us. I mean, having thought provoking poetry right after some pretty "graphic" (sex, they liked joking about sex) stand up kind of kills the vibe for some people who just want to laugh at dirty jokes all night (okay, maybe I'm throwing a bit of shade) without feeling like they have to go home and think about it. Which is understandable that we were asked very nicely to discontinue what we were doing there. And so, we did. At that point I could've taken that as a "Well, this was a nice ride for a month. Guess I'll go back to focusing on school and interning at Riverside Church", but thank God to that stubborn, resilient gut I've been given that said, "There has to be something else I can do." I just didn't know what that something else was...

Was it just sticking to doing poetry in church settings, adding to a culture that's already very exclusive or do I start something else? This is where my brother Anthony pushes me out of my comfort zone to start an open mic for poetry. Roaring Rhetoric was the name we thought up together. He did all the graphic designing for the ad and all the things on the production side. November 1, 2014 was the date of our first launch of Roaring Rhetoric; the open mic for poets in the community, co-founded by Anthony Flanigan and Aubrey Barnes. We didn't know where it was going to lead; whether it would die after a few months, or somehow live through the years. Would it have a small crowd of just us every month or would more people hear about this and attend? My friend Terence checked me in this season of my life and said to me "If folks don't give you a spot at the table, don't force a place at the table, but make your own damn table." So, with the correct carpentry skills, Roaring Rhetoric was made and still lives and breathe with great lungs! Started with an audience of eight, to this day being an audience of forty, and is the talk of the Quad Cities. It doesn't look like it has any intentions of-

Abandon Jesus to Find Jesus

"One of the most Christian things you could ever do is reject Jesus."

From 2014 till now, God has used poetry for more than what I expected it to be used for. Being an individual who believed in the historical account of Jesus and desired to do what I was called to do with my time here on Earth, I ate up and lived out everything preached to me by our westernized church culture. My sophomore year of college I started my first bible study group at Morningside College in Sioux City Iowa. I surrounded myself around people who were very devout in their faith, and we all sharpened each other as we say; encouraging each other to hold on to the faith with a tightly clenched fist with no indication of letting up. I thought I truly had everything about Christianity figured out. To me it looked like a checklist:

The Must Do's If You Claim To Love Jesus:
- Read your bible everyday
- Pray everyday
- Don't drink
- Don't smoke
- Don't cuss
- Don't have sex before marriage
- Start a bible study
- Read Christian Books
- Go to church every Sunday
- Go to small group every week
- Watch a sermon on YouTube on lunch breaks
- Have a devotional journal
- Go to retreats
- Don't go to bars
- Wear Christian Stuff

- Listen to Christian music ONLY
- Say "Jesus, God, Savior" at some point in your day
- Preach to lost souls about Jesus or else they will go to hell
- Start a blog talking about stuff only Christians will get
- Have Christian aspirations; plant a church, be a youth pastor, preacher, worship pastor
- Study apologetics heavily so you're ready for the day someone questions your faith
- Always smile
- Don't talk about your struggles
- Don't question the Bible, church, or pastors
- Don't be religious

For six years, I thought I was doing this Christian thing right with doing all these things correctly. I would never say that I wish I could redo anything in that time frame up until now, because it all was necessary for the perspective that poetry brought me. Poetry made, no, forced me to look at myself. It pushed me to admit my pride, rigidness, unspoken weaknesses, ignorance and dishonor at that. What I am about to say I don't say with the intention of being rebellious towards the church, nor do I desire people my age to start some fiery revolution of putting down church; that would be madly immature. With that said, Western Church culture taught me to remain within this culture of exclusivity; never stepping out into the real world, remain brainwashed and not think for myself, not to really venture that narrow path of realness, shadows, doubt, and suffering, but at the end find love, peace, and Jesus on a greater and more authentic level, outside of what we have made Christianity. God was teaching me to be healed from a sickness that I had been infected by for years; the need to please people. Even before I was serious about faith, everything I did was for the satisfaction of hearing accolades from people. Whether I had to excel at sports, be the life of the party on weekends, sleep with and manipulate the heart and emotion of girls. I did whatever needed to be done to feel accepted. This was no different in the church world, just had different terminology and tactics; get accepted by these pastors who love how much of a "Man of God" I was being, be a leader to all those young church attendants who loved how knowledgeable and Christian I was being. It was all to appease this deep need in me to be accepted and looked up too. I was doing art, poetry, while asking "how can I show how Christian I am?" During my pursuit of this hobby of poetry, I started catching the eye of the "other side"; people who didn't affiliate with religion. As a matter of fact, most of them hate it. But yet they were somehow drawn to what I was doing, and how I articulated things in poetry. I started having more opportunities laid out before me; doing shows at local coffee shops, bars, and going outside the state on tours with other artists. In this, God was showing me a world that he created outside of the world that we created. A world, full of people who bore his beautiful image, people who he loves dearly, people who have eyes that see something that overtly religious folks miss: that there is beauty in this world outside of our worldview. If we just took a step out by faith, we would be in awe of how God truly is in all things. I thank God for friends like Ryan Collins,

Beej Dillard, Gabe Cheng, Soultru; for organizations like the Midwest Writing Center, MadSkills, Nu-Gruv Society that God has used to change my whole perception of faith, God, Jesus, and the world. I thank God for the poetic advocates before me; Gil Scot Heron, Langston Hughes, Malcolm Guite, Propaganda, for they all showed me how to honor the art as well as authentically being myself. Entering into this year, 2017, as I sit behind this laptop, I live with this assurance, a quote I say to myself, "When you know who you is, you ain't worried 'bout who you is ain't." I am fully confident in who God has made me and what he is continually making me. I don't need to live for the acceptance of anybody, whether religious or on the completely opposite end. I am accepted in my skin right now, I am loved right now, I am forgiven right now. And for this, I have no other choice but to walk this world in thankfulness, love, and generosity. It may seem like I have found the answer, that I have found "The End", but while I am living on this Earth, my story, my struggles, my triumphs, my journey, and my Father God is unfin-

Unfin-

My story is unfin-
Unfin- as cracked concrete of hometown streets
Rock Island
Up way from Save-A-Lot where my story starts
But remains unfin-
Like the novel of my parents
A Mississippi foreigner and Illinois native
Who came together, wedded after couple months
acquainted
Then came me, two, three
Siblings who took a liking to wall scribbling
Some of those drawings remain unfin-
Like broccoli that sat on my plate
Only for few minutes for I didn't want it to be a cool
whip that I ate
Wooden spoons, extension cords put us in check
No privilege of threats, just belt tattoos that stung of
regret
Those butt whoopings never went unfin-
Like soiled pants
Dragon Ball Z planted priority over all bodily urgencies
So that number 1 emergency held on bus ride remained
inside
While I ran with the tenacity of Hermes towards home
Though such a goal was a failed mission, I accomplished
catching my show
We never thought Dragon Ball Z go unfin-
Like my urge for adventure
Driving my soul down giant gravel inclines on inline
skates

Past grandmama's crib during hot summer days
Tumbling terribly, carrying bloody bruises that burned under sun rays
Traveling at speeds that dropped jaws of concerning parents
There, I truly felt that no one could stop me
My yearning for journey will never go unfin-
Like backyard beat downs?
More like after school scuffles
Teaching me the psychology that was fight or flight
I couldn't fight, so only option was jet
Fly down sidewalks till I ran out of gas
Leaving me to see nosedive into grass
This routine would last from elementary to high school class
Whether being chased, or feeling out of place till problems were outran by my pace
But the race would go unfin-
As my love for running
Which never failed to turn grey skies to something sunny
I chased passion with pride, for a decade long
From state meets to national titles, my heart sung for running was my American Idol Yet I felt unfin-
Like my urge for validation
Doing anything to fill the voids in my soul
Whether it meant sneaking out past curfew
Dependent on Grey Goose and UV Blue
Clenched fists with airtight pressure
Pounding pupils till purple permeated
Till cold colt clasped in palm gave me calm
Till lust was fulfilled, and women swarmed

Till shame that lived was dead and gone
My journey for acceptance went unfin-
As school assignments
Shifting focus towards different tasks
Open bottles but bottled broken in flask
Women
Weaved wickedness within
Friends
Faintly falling, following foolishness, fleeing
Life
Looked lifeless, losing luster, lacking
Bible
My fortune cookie pocket book, pen, pad, poetry
Produced pleading pain filled prayers to pass parched
lips
I wanted God to not let life feel unfin-
Unlike his finished work on the cross
Jesus, a name I knew but never knew, this was new
It was like Hope became an Assembly
That desperate feet would run to after class
And Sunday mornings soon as sun met day
Scripture was no more a book of philosophies
Good luck ideologies
It checked hearts of young and old at door
It desired to ID all OGs
It's wisdom would never be unfin-
Unalike my old nature
Calls from God's Goodness ended rings from rebellion
New doors open, old friends found exits
Eyes and feet past me as if I didn't exist
He gained my soul, I lost the world

Thank God some friendships remained unfin-
As The Great Commission
A mission that changed mind's intuition
Craving to tell about His Crucifixion
Whether in front of pews of pious peoples
Or spitting truth for those who've never seen a steeple
For my children so they will stand in stance of David
and fear no evil
To my brothers and sisters who run with me, causing
hell upheaval
I pray that the Spirit's
work may never go
unfin- Unfin- in my old
bones, when this flesh
becomes weak
As I rock in my old wooden chair that meets floors with
a squeak
Peering, old eyes out toward sunset
Reminiscing on all things that the Son had set
From that chair my left hand shall grasp my wife's
While right raises towards ceiling
Giving God gratitude for taking our lives on that Cross
Proclaiming, "it is finished" so soul would not go lost
This story that you hear, every day that this breathe
decide to give cheer
Until death gets its sucker punch, and my grave draws
near
Know that the Lord is still painting
Illustrating His image in me
My story, our stories
Let's not be worried with how they'll en-

Spitology?

Before we embark any further with this journey, I want to introduce a new word to you good folks. A word that I accredit to my boy Jeremiah. Say it with me now; one, two, three... "Spitology"! There you go, your pronunciation was astounding! The Spitology is like the host to the guest artist, the headliner to the main act, the narrator to the main character! In these sections, you will get the idea, event, situation that brought the poem to be. There is nothing that cannot spark the imagination of the human mind, and give way to the human soul to express itself. I hope these small stories humor you, touch you, provoke thought, and prick your heart with something great. With that said, let's go on with the show!

Color

"I look to a day when people will not be judged by the color of their skin, but by the content of their character." – Martin Luther King Jr.

Spitology – Black Like Me

If you are a fan of my work, I bet my bottom dollar that you would've skipped all other poems for this one... Which is why I cleverly decided to put this one at the front of the book! Out of all my pieces that i've written, I never thought this one would be as popular as it has turned. It's awkward, it's funny. It will inspire you, it will offend you. Either way, you will be impacted by my life experiences, which is what this poem is an accumulation of. Growing up in Rock Island, I felt as if I was stuck within a paradox that we are all familiar with in some way. Being an African American who wasn't cultured deemed me an oddity. And the synonym for oddity to those who called me out? White. Meaning, though I was physically, visibly, skin pigmentation proven to be black, I really was white. Want to know where it gets even more confusing? In high school, I dated a young lady from Geneseo Illinois, where I encountered a whole different world. To put it this in a slightly comical and serious way, the residents weren't very fond of those whose skin was naturally darker than their farmboy tans. I remember the first time I started dating this girl, the principal at her school emailed her mother, informing her that her daughter was hanging out with someone that was "bad news". I had moments where I would be hanging out with my girlfriend's friend's friend's house, only to have hours of awkward, unnecessary, quiet tension because the friends refused to talk to me. As a matter of fact, like the few encounters with people in Geneseo, they hated my entire being! Why? Simple (sort of...); I was black. So, yep. I am black, and white, like a zebra.... Or a Panda....

Or, my favorite, a flipping oreo! Though I now look at this and laugh, because it is obviously a super ridiculous concept, it hurts me deeply at the same time. Not for myself, but for those who feel trapped by these propagated notions preached by culture that says black people must "this", or they are out. No exceptions. If we're honest, our need to label people due to these things is a mirror of our deeper problem of trying to understand the what can't be understood. If we can't understand it, we grow confused, frustrated at ourselves, and maybe even deeply envious of those who broke out the box of social expectations, and decided to be what they were made to be, not what people wanted them to be.

"In Christ's family, there can be no division into Jew and non-Jew, slave and free, male and female. Among us you are all equal. That is, we are all in a common relationship with Jesus Christ." - Paul

"The human race has one effective weapon, and that is laughter." - Mark Twain

Black Like Me

Let me tell you a fact about myself that almost everyone
I meet feels the need to remind me
I am black
I'm so black that I make Micheal Blackson not seem so
Black, son
I'm so black that in a game of laser tag I should be
permitted to keep my
Eyes open and teeth showing, otherwise i'd be cheating
I'm so black that you would swear that i'm a vampire
Because when i'm in photos with no flash, all you see
floating clothes
I'm so black that when I go out for a run
People look at me in jaw dropping awe
Speechless that I'm moving so fast
They mistake me for the Flash
But, he's a white superhero so that'd never happen
Instead they look at me in grandiose curiosity, asking
"Sir, are you from Africa?"
I'm so black that when I mention that I like to watch
basketball
People roll their eyes to a point that i'd swear their
brain rolled right along with them
But when I go to games in cities such as Geneseo
You would swear that I walked into the Gymnasium in
my underwear
The way people silently over stare
At me
The odd black man at a basketball game
He must be here for a girl

Or to cause some trouble
Maybe we should make eye contact when he doesn't
make eye contact
But if he makes eye contact when we make eye contact
He'll knock our eye contacts
Out
Let's just not make any contact
I am so black that my teammate in college was stricken
with fear at my appearance
But when he heard that my speech was "politically
correct"
And my posture was erect, he breathed out in great
calm
Because it was evident that I was
White
So white that I make Carleton seem like Tupac
So white that I mistaken Malcolm X's name for Malcolm
the Tenth
So white that when someone asks me if I got green on
me
I think i'm getting robbed
I am so white that my all white friend, from an all white
college
In an all white city told me
"You aren't like the black people on TV"
When I play basketball, people run to me for a challenge
And leave the victor, easy 21 to my hard toiled 16
Saying "you must not have inherited it in your genes"
But as for rapping
When it comes to these sixteens
I'm sweet like i'm sixteen
Addictive like nicotine

Spit that fire like kerosene
And you know what friends say to me?
"Oh my gosh, you actually are black!"
So I am black
But I am White
Or maybe people are just color blind
Shutter blinds closed to any sunny possibility of a no label society
Globular organs shrouded with stereotypical presumptions
Assumptions derived from contrived corruptions
Making these ideas of "acting black" and "acting white" as alright
But it's not alright if you're white acting black
Or black acting white
Well it is okay
Just know we're going to give you a hard time
When you forgot your belt at home, making your pants a little
We're going to say you're dressing black
Or when your belt is around your waist and nicely fit
We're going to then say you dress 'white'
Kind of like how Pharisees, those religious leaders you hate
Judged good and evil by what they perceived with their eyes
Instead of looking into the heart that lies
When Eloheim said there is no Jew nor Gentile
Nor male or female
I believe if he stood in the midst of our color-coded community
He would say there is no black nor white

I am exactly what I was destined to be
An oddity and comedy
Laughable because giggling only makes sense of
something that doesn't make sense
A black acting white, a white acting black
An oxymoron that gives minds prone to label panic
attacks
No one goes to an ice cream store because the flavors
are all the same
That'd be lame
Just like a Matrix filled with agents, the Neos bring
change
Something out the norm
So i'll forever say i'm
The paint splashes in a padded room
That can't be cleaned by swiffer, rag or a broom
I am what I am Because I Am said I am
So you see
It's not that I am whiter than you
Or you're blacker than me
But we're the same
Human beings bearing the same beautiful image
So in the end, i'm white like you
And you're black like me

Spitology – Black Like Me, Too

When I wrote this part two for Black Like Me, I was in a place of brutal honesty of how these racial issues affect me. Having a majority of friends that are white, there were little things that always bugged me. Things that weren't their fault, because they weren't aware of the weight of their words. From little jokes like, "Aubrey, you're the whitest black guy i've ever met", from comments taking root out of serious issues, "well maybe if he (a black person) didn't live in the ghetto, he'd be where you are!". Though none of the comments or little bits of banter weren't meant to be harming to anyone, they made me feel inadequate; always reminding me that no matter the content of my character, I was still pigeon holed with all other minorities. I was looked at no different from the lady walking down the street who has a fear of minorities, or to the individual coming from high socioeconomic standards of living who saw all minorities as lazy. I know the butt hurt tendencies people get when someone seems to 'play victim', so I thought about the other side. Don't take my saying "butt hurt" as having only a motivation of not making white people angry as the goal. Writing the other narrative that minorities don't really think about was a good challenge for me. It put me in a place of not thinking about my scars, my hurts as much, and think about my neighbor's feelings of inadequacy. In a world where white cops are heavily ridiculed and hated by minorities, and white women are objectified in the culture of hip hop, there are much apologies to make, and scars to bandage. In and of that, I realized this; that if we all dropped our rigid defensive walls built from inadequacy and fear, we would see that our perceived 'enemy' on the other end is just as scared and weak as we are. When I look at it through that perspective, I have no choice but to run to that antagonist and embrace him. Fix up his or her wounds, and let them know they mean something. That may sound like the most unrealistic, hippie, liberal thing that you have ever heard. And that's okay.

"You know exactly how I was made, bit by bit,
   how I was sculpted from nothing into something." -
David the Psalmist

"The reason why the world lacks unity, and lies broken and in heaps, is, because man is disunited with himself." - Ralph Waldo Emerson

Black Like Me, Too

I often feel inadequate
Many of you don't know this feeling
Like all you have to offer this world is in accord to
stereotypes
Where questions like,
"What's your favorite color?"
"Will you be my best friend?"
That were once asked out of childlike innocence
Have been shaped by hands of cynicism and sarcasm
Designed to cleverly cage culture with cunning curiosity
"Do you rap?"
"Can you dance?"
And if you passion for anything of this fashion
You qualify yourself to walk their runway of shame
Becoming the butt of black jokes
As snickers circle your ebonics and cultural
colloquialisms
Which are foreign, foolish, and filthy
To society's sterilized prescriptive grammar globe
So if you is choppin' it up wit' yo folks who be woke
Talmbout how dem J's is dope
Yo intelligence be irrelevant
Cuz it's assumed that yo lack of linguistics deserves pity
From those convinced that you're the problem
In their opinion
If you valued police compliance
Exercised rights to remain silent
There'd be no worry about getting shot
Nor seeing riots

35

And church folks turn
backs on black issues
Preaching a colorblind
rhetoric that says:
Ignore differences all together
Believing that their black cousin
Or dark skinned BFF has enlightened them
Disagreeing that there's white privilege at all
And in turn
Remain holy and homogenous
I've felt these pains
Accustomed to being the elephant in suburban town
church buildings
Amongst many Caucasian brothers and sisters
Who have probably driven through the ghetto
But never intentionally walked its streets
Grafted souls to blood stained sidewalks
Run hands over beautifully spray canned murals of the
broken
Yet sit comfortably in circles of Kumbaya
Discussing what's wrong with God's church
When I know peers peering through bullet blotched
windows
Dying in the hood without hope
Though I bite my tongue
Knowing that if I share worries within the theater of my
mind
I'll be labeled Ludacris
Leaving others to flip the script
Accusing me of playing victim
When the way "my people" act is the problem
So i've stopped searching for solutions

Awkwardly laugh when late as friends joke about me
running on "CP" time
Giggling
Trying to make sense of feeling that don't make sense
Then I find this penny for my thought
That you also feel inadequate
With an inadequacy that I can't ever relate with
Like all you have to offer this world is in accord to
stereotypes
Where questions that were once asked out of innocence
Have been shaped by hands of ignorance and
obstinance
Designed to cleverly cage your culture
"Whos yo favorite country singer?"
Is yo parents rich?
Is you rich?
And if you happen to have cheese
Great, we've shredded you over our assumptions
Nicknaming you "that one white kid"
As if no other characteristics matter
Unless you're that white kid that raps
Living in the trap, playing craps
Convincing ourselves that you look like Eminem
Though freckles frolic face like a field fire
With hair follicles as red as a Cardinal's feathers
And women are given the hardest time
Seen as prey to us young-minded predators
With confidence placed in our onyx skin
That makes us bolder
Believing that every young lady wants to rock wit us
And if you turn down our request to kick it

Claiming we have no game
Unable to play cards right
And you're over 21
We bust out in shame
And claim it's 'cause we're black, jack
We can't forget teachers
Selflessly accepting inner city placements
Only to hand out "F's", then be deemed a racist
Though students choose not to study on a daily basis
And never forsake noble police officers
Who take heat for lousy deputies
Burning under glares of hate
From those of different ethnicity
Who view them all as enemies
As if every cop has the urge to stop
Pop and imprison every black skinned boy and girl
This feeling, I will never know
Though youthful ignorance would've told me so
From elementary years that brought many tears
To high school days of being called "white boy" by peers
Teased, tackled, torn apart
Topsy turvy to why i'm too black to befriend
And too white to hang out with on weekends
Even with all my playground experiences
That chucked wood chips in weeping eyes
I'd never understand the planks pressed in yours
But I don't have too
I don't have to experience, nor point out difference
To love you through oblivion
Because the Son of man merged Jews and Gentiles
Parting pride and prejudice through his blood so red

See, we don't need to feel offended
Nor exhaust brains with ways to reach a culture
But realize that we all feel inadequate
We all are broken
And we all need to know love, dearly
As I realize this, I have no choice but to conclude
That I'm white like you
And you're black like me
Too

Spitology – Faces

Sometimes in the heat of the moment, in the heat of taking offense and defense in the battle of who's right and who's wrong, we forget about the things that most deserve our attention. As I mentioned earlier, July was a month of much unnecessary bloodshed. During a riot in Dallas in response to police brutality that transpired, a few officers who were attempting to calm down the rioters ended up getting shot and killed by a sniper. These officers, who were humans like the rest of us; humans who lived, breathed, and had loved ones, were faintly mentioned and are hardly remembered to this day. The victims of police brutality are forever engraved within the minds of many, but these officers and their names deemed foreign. Not only that, but their deaths were celebrated; seen as the product of payback by an angry black community, justifying this act of vengeance. As I remembered these officers, I thought of them no different than those who fell victim by officers. As I read their stories, I thought of them no different than Alton Sterling or Philando Castile. They were humans who died in the most unfortunate, unnecessary way. If we were able to see the faces of the victims we speak about in such ill manner; have dinner with them, befriend them, hear their story, we'd realize the beautiful humanity that they are. How they are more than a product of bloody revenge, or a statistic of a history of crime. If we saw their faces for what they were, humans worthy of life and dignity, maybe we'd grieve more and fight less. Maybe we would vulnerably love more and defensively fight less. Every face we see on a daily basis, even for a second, is a face that has a great story behind it. If we should see that face again or never ever see it again, we can praise the Image that it reflects, and the story God has crafted through it.

"Jesus wept." - Author of John's Gospel

"In times of grief and sorrow I will hold you and rock you and take your grief and make it my own. When you cry I cry and when you hurt I hurt. And together we will try to hold back the floods to tears and despair and make it through the potholed street of life." - Nicholas Sparks

Faces

I see faces
Faces I probably won't face tomorrow
Fearfully, wonderfully shaped in a Shepherd's image
Before sun sets, let's tell them how son rose for every
broken image bearing face
In case we don't see that face tomorrow
I grieve for him
He didn't know his destination tomorrow would be not
here
That fellows he never followed would tweet about him
As if they knew him since knee high
As if Facebook and Fox news told of his triumphs
And not just his fatal fall
As breath returns last borrow to atmosphere
Pressed out with a pistol's kiss
Arms, fighting to rise like a boxer buried by body shots
Trembling, meeting harsh reality's persuasion of defeat
As blood stained body hangs over passenger seat like
ropes around ring
While babies watched from backseat
Silent like vocal chords rewired themselves to irises
that day
Making pain spill from eyelids without audibles
Daddy was never a fan of murder films
But these poor children experienced their first 3D, up
close real time view
Of R rated content
Youngins unaware their family would be another sad
statistic
For sociologists, acting as prophets

Professing a broken future due to devastating past
As my eyes meet faces
Smiling cheeks of dark daddy's' carrying daughters on strong shoulders
I am reminded that I possibly won't see them tomorrow
Faces shaped in a Shepherd's image, fearfully, wonderfully made
Before the sun sets, let's tell them how the son rose for every broken image bearing face
In case we don't see that face tomorrow
I grieve for them
They didn't know they'd lie under loafers of loved ones tomorrow
That fellows they never met would continue not to know them
As if just 'cause their patriotic lights flash same on vehicles
All their stories illuminate similarly
As News headlines accumulated names
Converting and unifying them to one number
As if their names didn't carry with them stories
Novels on how that badge burned with nobility
Years of late night crams for final exams were pages worth citing
Decades of fighting for country were chapters worth reading
Even till end of fearlessly fighting
Though lips would never make way to children's heads for good nighting
They never knew that they'd be the ones tucked in indefinitely

While compassions from colored community was closed in caskets
These officers had families
Were laymen, newlyweds, veterans
Brent Thompson, Patrick Zamarripa, Michael Krol
Michael Smith, Lorne Ahrens, Gretchen Rocha and many
Died serving Dallas
Their integrity illuminates through our officers
Serving without expectation of being served
Turning cheeks when slapped with assumptions
Going two miles for those who desire only one
They deserve our cup of cold water
For we aren't as different as we claim to be
We're faces
Image bearers that are but a vapor
Here a moment, dissipated the next
Let's remember each other's faces
Yearn to learn each other's story
And before the sun sets, let's reminisce on how the son rose
Loving each other for his spirit lets us so

Spitology – It's Simple

Everybody has some kind of opinion on everything when they get behind a keyboard. Catch those same people anywhere else in public, their confidence and boldness miraculously disappears in every way. When police brutality caused the up rise of this organization called "Black Lives Matter", I swear everyone in the world had something to say about it or against it. All I saw on my Facebook were five minute videos of 'experts' explaining why police were just in ending a life of whoever the person was at the time, people posting memes attacking each other with dishonorable satire, and alas someone (who probably had good intentions, hopefully) thought it would be smart to remind everyone in the world at this time that "#AllLivesMatter". Facebook, Twitter, and all other social media outlets were places of great race war. It was madly ridiculous. One night, I fell to the urge to pursue a 'conversation' with a friend from Minnesota who said "Black Lives Matter is a ridiculous organization... Stop being stupid around cops, it's simple" (paraphrased). Thought I didn't stand with what the organization stood for, I understood the heart of fear and despair that it came out of. I also do understand (though very little will admit to it), whenever people see a title of something that starts with the word "black", anything that smells of racial divide, they start getting defensive and feel the need to say something on the lines of, "well if that said "White" that wouldn't be right, would it?" So, I wrote this poem as a response to this friend. We all wish that unfortunate social issues were simple to solve, not just on the race issue side of things. We all wished that logic could solve all things, but it can't. Our knowledge, our savvy internet studies on statistics and essays on social issues to back up our bias have the capacity to make us bigger jerks to one another, and contribute nothing but a bigger hole. Most of the time a super self-righteous, politically charged answer isn't what is needed, but just radical love and compassion to our neighbors.

".... We know that "We all possess knowledge." But knowledge puffs up while love builds up." – Paul

It's Simple

All Lives Matter, it's just that simple
Simple as one plus one
Unless one grabs a gun 'cause the other one reached for
wallet
And pulls trigger as if borrowing bullets from a
neighboring number
Forgetting its job was to add not subtract, but let's look
at facts
I mean Chris Rock said it best
Don't be stupid and you won't be shot dumb
So if you reach for pocket, the boys in blue will stop it
But don't dare bring up facts as well
Like Joseph Houseman who left his house manning a
rifle
Whose nose pointed towards police like it needed a
kleenex
And they were there just in time to get blown into
But never once was he shot into
So I guess it isn't that simple
But it has to be that simple
Simple like raising hands and asking for help in class
Picture police as your teacher
Whose also Simon
So if Simon says raise hands
Play his tune like a one man band
But don't bring up that one fellow's name
Gilbert Flores
Whose heart probably felt like a fear-stricken child
surrounded by wolves

Eyes pacing and shaking like a weary marathon
runner's legs
Pupils burning as tension's sweat seared them
As arms extended up like the arms extended out
towards him
Strained and still as if he knew his next steps would be
before God
Hoping that his forced worship redeemed his soul
Orchestrated by religious folks
Who were good at playing God with their gavel like
guns
That were so quick to point and pop judgement
Dropping dear Gilbert like the sweat's last dance from
his brow
So I guess it isn't that simple
But it has to be that simple
Simple like getting straight A's on report cards
No different than keeping a clean record
Follow the law to the T
Don't speed, drive while texting
And even the extremes
Like selling people weed
Yeah, even if you happened to be pulled over
With record being reach back two decades
During that one summer at age 16
When your older cousin manipulated you to back pack
his beretta
Leading to your felony
Cutting you off from longevity
You should've grew up where I did
Your parents parenting apparently paved present
mistakes inherently

So now you're inheriting the seed they sowed so
carelessly
I have never heard of a cop who wasn't kind hearted
So this racism should be disregarded
It's that simple
So simple that it ain't simple
We all wished it was like acne
So need only be proactive to pop it's pimple
But this dermatitis has been
inflaming since sixteen hundreds
How can you have already figured
it out?
You haven't
You're a liar
Lying on a lumpy tempur pedic of self-consciousness
Building defenses derived from pointed fingers
Your "All Lives Matter" was generated out of
misconceptions
Seeing our lament as a divisive creed
Coming to our funerals where faces fill with grieving
and praying lips
As you command us to #JustForgetIt
We all have family members who die
His death meant nothing
His murder meant little
All lives matter spill black lives liquid
Dumping tears down street drains
Please leave your biases by door
And embrace our pain
Hug us tight and tell us it will be alright
Though it ain't that simple
Love is that simple

That's all we ask for

Spitology – Interracial

I was hanging out with one of my good friend's and his wife one night, and we got into this conversation of interracial relationships. How we ended up there? Can't even remember. You see my friend is black and his wife is white, and with this relationship they've had a few awkward run ins. People who saw them and their kids would grow angry, resentful, and downright judgmental because they weren't of the same race. It's really funny when you think about it, to think that people are only allowed to date and marry other people of their own race and ethnicity. As I reflected on the conversation and my own experiences, this poem came out of it all.

"I believe in recognizing every human being as a human being--neither white, black, brown, or red; and when you are dealing with humanity as a family there's no question of integration or intermarriage. It's just one human being marrying another human being or one human being living around and with another human being." - Malcolm X Interracial

Interracial

To the elderly woman at the grocery store
I noticed your glare of disapproval
As you noticed me
Skin dark as moonless skies
And my wife
Containing a complexion white as cloud clustered
firmaments
As our fingers bonded like vows that tied knots
You wished your bones weren't so feeble
So you could undo such undignified union
Your hate was scalding water running from lips
Out your tea kettle mouth
As ears whistled
Steam spewing so sincerely
Our unity rattled your bones to core
As if dread found way through navel passage
Making you shake with every attempt to place canned
items on belt
You claim it is out of anger
But your demeanor screams confusion
Baffled by how two worlds can fusion dance
Despite pointed fingers of past
Historic hate and disunion
I wanted to tell you about Jesus
How though your heart be black
He yearns to wrap his Grace as white as snow
'Round your cold shoulders
Rolling your stone hard heart away like the boulder
blocking his burial bed

You yearn for an interracial relationship
To the young man at the mall
Passing glances past my queen
I noticed your glare
So infatuated
Fantasizing assumptions so good
In fact you at it
Consumed every philosophy received from
rhymesayers,
Naysayers
Saying white women are like drive thrus
If you're thirsty
Just drive thru
And they'll fill your cup to brim for cheap
Regardless if their boss man arches over like a water
fountain
'Cause these hoes ain't loyal
I wanted to meet and greet jaw with jarring jabs
And fracture your favorite Emcees ribs
For painting such a fowl picture of my fiance
But it goes beyond say
That if I were a boy
I'd be crazy in love with all the single ladies
And unsingle
You're just drunk in, lust
I wanted to tell you about Jesus
How because of him, girls don't run your world
So you don't have to objectify
Pacify pictures
Painted by perverted Picassos
But know that a Man dyed black with white

To whitewash wickedness from your riddled canvas
You yearn for an interracial relationship
To the pompous white waiter, I noticed your glare of disbelief
As you sat them at their table
White man with his black wife
A product of a very misfortunate blind date you say
Or maybe the man is an innocent bystander
To this woman with pickaxe nails
Ready to gold dig when opportunity surfaced
The subtle shock on your face was laughable
When ears heard that they were married
It was as if a new world was at feet
Where Yin and Yang can actually intertwine
Where moon and sun could actually align
And not create darkness
But a beautiful light of hope
How I wish I could have told you about Jesus
And how though he could've stayed among heavenly hosts
He chose to be us
Touching, healing our our deepest wounds
No matter the ethnicity
Feed us with the little he had
No matter our race
And one day be our groom
No matter the color of our face
You were made
for an
interracial
relationship

Spitology – Write Privilege

Being an African American, I count it nothing short of a great blessing and privilege to walk this path that was paved through great efforts by my ancestors. Even before African slaves were taught how to read or write, they would hum beautiful work songs to each other in the fields of work. Some slave masters taught their slaves to read and write, while others had to sneak around and find ways of obtaining these skills; whether that meant sneaking off into the night and take books from the master's house, or wait for those slaves who put their life on the line to travel to different slave plantations to teach others the skills they acquired. Once this power was grasped and mastered, the world saw a great and powerful movement of storytelling, music, and poetry that would forever catch the eyes of European people. They were astonished, blown away, and many tried to oppress them all the more because blacks finally came to a place of consciousness; not just spiritually now, but intellectually. They became a force to be reckoned. From the early 1600s of slavery to the 1930s of the Harlem renaissance which birthed many intellectual and artistic figures in the African American culture. Song writing, poetry, and storytelling were used not just for entertainment, but to spark a revolution of change; to turn the narrative of oppression and segregation that the United States was adopting. The artist was not about himself or herself, but advocates of encouragement toward their oppressed brothers and sisters; igniting a flame within them that would carry onto others for years to come. Now we're here in 2017 with the original leaders of this movement passed away, but their voices still alive through the arts. If you're like me, after realizing the beauty that birthed art, it feels like some have lost the purpose of it all. We're less about encouraging others and more about just saying whatever comes to mind. Whether that be misogynistic, violent, divisive, or whatever it may be, the heart behind music and art has become calloused I don't want to come off as if I am a one-sided pro-black advocate, I just realize the responsibility of those before us who made it possible to even experience art. Art liberates, challenges, and pushes against the woodwork. Art is willing to have its own bloodshed for the best. Art in that sense is practically synonymous to God, which is why I think it is such a powerful force. When we know and experience art in its true naked roots, we find a greater identity to be lived out and expressed in a world where identity is being grabbed at on a daily basis.

"Hold fast to dreams, For if dreams die, Life is a broken-winged bird, That cannot fly." – Langston Hughes

Write Privilege

I always wondered why they wrote
And all they wrote about was race
Ancestors illiterate hands wrote stories with tongues
As voices shifted stars to illustrations
Work songs and field hollers healed pain pressed at
backs
Illiteracy never stopped slaves from seeking to learn
Tricking children of masters to teach them how to
master sentences
While other owners openly educated servants
Unaware that these would be keys to shackles
A Spirit that would soar and saturate solar systems
Breathe life into literature like lilac's aroma carried in
wind
Dropping jaws of white writers who wrote their stories
Birthing Phillis Wheatley's passion for poetry
Frederick Douglass who wrote letters to his master
Their stories were bleeding scars turned to healing
hope
Eyes that saw a future free and equal
Knowing that pen and pad were more than producers of
poetry for public
But a walking stick and sandals for a journey
Whose end was never seen, but felt
Independence would be sought in the pen dent
Not with clinched fists, but quill feathers fashioned with
ink
Writing till they cease all fighting
I always wondered why they wrote
And all they wrote about was race

Harlem Renaissance renegades
Rebelling unrighteousness through writings
World war sacrifices didn't end vices
Poverty and unemployment didn't stop a celebration of culture
Cultivating art so ambidextrously embodying harsh realities upon paper as finger tips press pen
While other hand uplifts weight from weary shoulders
Langston Hughes reminded others that he was America too
Maya Angelou wrote about Willie's days
Who lived in the games children play
These artists didn't paint poetry for profit and popularity
Not just for entertainment but to see freedom from enslavement
And when stock markets brought Great Depression
Writing became meal ticket to starving artists
Vagabonds shoved between publication or fight for nation that noosed ya
Spit in faces would be a soldier's congratulations
Their stories were tall story buildings of Wall Street
Working, writing just to break past first floor
Sweating under white lights to discover black power
Pounding past Jim Crow with marching feet to bullets that fleet
Those who spoke up laid down foundation for freedom
I wonder why we write
And why we don't write about the right race
It's like we lost view of our forerunner and found our own path
Gold chains shackle us again

Empty bullets by roadside alongside weapons long
abandoned
Like the children we brag about not being our blood
Yet we validate our art that aggravates by our struggle
that necessitates
Our project based, drug solicited society are our stories
Endorsing our novels like as if negativity was our savior
Praising drug lords, baptizing broken peoples in
champagne
Painting pictures only for profit and popularity
Crafting only what will fill pockets and portfolios
Whether it be misogyny or moving packs
Or bragging about cops dodged while stacking racks
Yet grow angered when life is lost by these lifestyles
We've forgotten their stories
Writers, warriors who fought to give God glory
David wrote a buck fifty worth of poetry
Jesus wrote stories on the tablet adjacent to sternums
And ancestors wrote about our race
Whose finish line is our finished line
Our verses, our bars, our stanzas
Are what break stereotypes and statistics of spectators
This race needs runners who will carry torches of our
descendants
Who alter and amend our amendments
Who don't overemphasize superficial things
But remind us of our identity as kings and queens
Uplift the child on 11th street corner
Embrace black beauties who believe to be nothing but
Bodies to bear bruises and brokenness from brothers
This pen is our fight privilege
This pad gives new sight privilege

This voice and beating heart hold light privilege
When at disadvantages
Remember our long fought write privilege

Spitology – Kryptonite

There are a few words that instantly make me upset pretty quick. Okay, maybe only two. The "B" word (depending on context), and the word "ghetto". Whenever I hear the word ghetto being used by friends or other people i've had conversations with, it's used with a negative connotation in mind; either in describing a person or a place, or the characteristics someone has. "That store is so ghetto", "That person is so ghetto", and my favorite, "that neighborhood is so ghetto". The definition of the word ghetto is a part of a city that is occupied by a minority group. In our use of it today, it is used to describe something run down, impoverished, ignorant, and dangerous. I remember the last conversation I had with my ex-fiance as we were deciding where to hold our reception. The place that I was looking at was in an area that she described as ghetto; explaining that the people walking around the neighborhood are scary, and her relatives would not feel safe parking their cars around such an area. And this is why I chose to break the engagment. Jokes! But jokes aside, in all reality her outlook on neighborhoods that are unfamiliar, and people groups who were not prevalent in her upbringing was not something that was intentionally offensive but a product of assumption and fear. Stereotypes in movies, fictional television shows, and national news can create an negative and fictitious view. In turn, we walk on eggshells around certain people, hold ideas of neighborhoods that create safe boundaries to keep from being harmed. And the result of that is a broken view of other racial groups within racial groups. Black folks think white people don't care about them, hispanic groups stay within their racial boundaries, and european folks don't understand the privilege and lack of when it comes to skin color. Everyone remains ignorant to the other. When I see Jesus, I see someone who was not afraid to break boundaries. I see a man who wasn't afraid to ask a samaritan woman for water; which was a racial boundary that wasn't to be crossed back then. Jesus' love for people propelled him to mute out the distraction of fear, and give himself to those who were crying and pleading for help. The urban neighbors in our world, the 'hood', the 'ghetto', are fearful places because we have made them that way. In reality, they are no different than anywhere else; just a place with broken people who deserve vulnerable, authentic love like anywhere else.

"No sunshine or feeling better (the ghetto)
Watch em all scatter they'll kill each other (the ghetto)
If yo daddy dead, can't make him proud in (the ghetto)
Damn little boy, how you make it out of (the ghetto)" -
King Los (The Ghetto)

Kryptonite

I remember my first time
Seeing a dead body
Resting
In a bed of snow
Corpse covered by cold sheets
Blankets built up over body
As he slumbered in strange solitude
His face? Solid dude
Forehead held tension
As if mind attempted
To bench press nightmares
That weighed him down
His cheeks so blue
It was like he never learned
How to take totes of breath between reps
So ribs became bankrupt
To oxygen debt
The irony of it
He met his fate by moving weight
For a client who played spotter
And chose to drop pounds to chest
With impact penetrating past breast
Now he lay breathless
I wondered in perplexment
Where Superman was
Why phone booths in uphill suburbia
Weren't existent in this neighborhood
I wondered where Clark Kent was

Bewildered by why he didn't fly to our rescue
Stand in way of slugs
So we didn't take an "S" to chest
Why wasn't he there to carry kids within' arms
Like he did Lois lane
Swooping them out of path of speeding cars
Instead leaving long grieving mothers
Driven to depression in lowest lane
Does his heart drop quicker
Than his descension from Krypton
When he sits behind desk during day job
Printing reports in heavy ink
Of another man killed in a blink of an eye
The speed he could travel from east to southside
Stopping one less
obituary from being
orchestrated So
with all this
considered I wanted
to know why Clark
can't?
They said the answer was simple
Just notice how travelers
Cautiously border concrete jungles
Like public zoos whose animals
Are far from tamed
Parents pull kids close in cowardice
Women grip gucci underarms
With great offensive force
Television has ways of
Making monkeys of men
Showing spectators only

The horror stories of hood
Villains opposing what's good
Children cased in caskets of wood
No hero would save if he could
I've always hated the term ghetto
It always made things read backwards
Yes warsaw was raw
He would deliver reviled wickedness
But no devil lived on
Our neighborhoods
Don't treat 'em as same
Just' cause area I live is twisted evil
But uphill is held high in esteem
While downs deemed damnation
Justification for modification
To alter specification by gentrification
So petrification pauses crime
With stone cold gaze
That's what mighty Medusa uses
As a matter of fact
It's the mighty med U.S.A. uses
That powerful pill
Solution to sickness
Though docs repel lepers
Unwilling to get to heart issue
Dig past scar tissue
To see how to save civilians
Leaving homes hopeless
Seeing the hero in heroine
Trusting in Luke Cage to come
I mean nuke cane to numb

Paranoia of prison
Or voice in head considering wrist slitting
Or crooks contemplating house lifting
Or Gun flipping
Or son's missing
Or police blame shifting
This place isn't the most glamorous i'll admit And
Superman may much rather grasp kryptonite
With closed tight fists
Than draw some blood from crip tonight
But think tonight
Did Jesus ever avoid the Canaanite?
Deny a dog a simple bite
When others denied her appetite?
If not, why do people look at concrete jungle in fearful
bewilderment?
Didn't John's voice cry from wilderness?
Calling civilized to submit to baptism's tenderness?
For better temperament?
He didn't do this in safe secure sanctuaries
Nor did Jesus avoid adversaries
But walked barefoot through brokenness
Hung with the marginalized
Punished and pulverized
Hung for the colonized
It should be no surprise
That compared to such a savior
Why one would be led to lose faith in
Superheroes

Spitology – Gunplay

Many unfortunate events happened in 2016 within the month of July. From police brutality to brutality upon police, it seemed as if the world was falling apart. And close to home, events were devastating as well. A young teenage girl was shot and killed by two teen boys in July. I remember seeing all this, and growing troubled; troubled by artists aesthetically gifted who weren't able to realize or believe the power and influence they had over people groups. I saw families torn to bits emotionally to the reality of relatives being murdered, while in the Westside Chicago area, this subgenre within rap called drill music was becoming popular with many around the world; a style of rap that's only focus was praising street violence and murder, endorsing it to many who listened. I am a firm believer that art in and of itself can't answer for every political and social woe, but I do believe in its power to either turn malicious tides or create people who are comfortable with riding the waves. This poem, for me, was and still is an attempt for my people to do the uncomfortable work of challenging our own culture where it needs to be. Not with an iron fist and a condemning heart, but more so with a posture that says, "we've had enough. We are better than what we've identified ourselves as for the last fifty years. Let's better our communities, and empower each other".

"We may never be strong enough to be entirely nonviolent in thought, word and deed. But we must keep nonviolence as our goal and make strong progress towards it" – Mahatma Ga

Gunplay

Blood spill is glorified by dark hands daily
Its vicious cycles been spinning wheels
Since 1986 in the Mornin', frigid as Ice-T
When rap wrapped teeth round fruit flourishing from
good and evil
Opening eyes to knowledge to pay homage too
Exalting smoking shells, praising friends that paid bail
Exalting smoking shells, praising friends that paid bail
Exalting smoking shells, praising friends that paid bail
Its vicious cycles been spinning wheels
Peddling poison IVs through veins
Pumping premeditated murder to minds
Creating a culture that continues to increase influence
Making disciples doomed to martyrdom
Students who can't stand gospel music
But listen to Church in these streets
As preachers preach through subsystems
Saying God so loved the world
That he sent subs and snub nose to sons
To blast both bully and bystanders
Manipulating youth to perish people before eternal life
is explored
Deceived by their three sixteens
Craving to grow up gun blazin
Before we question police brutality
Before we answer back with marches and protest
Let's picket sign press these artists who swear they go
the hardest
Like where was your presence when cold steel pressed
heat through hearts

Brothers blasting forth and back, black on black crime
We heard your music between shots
Lyrics lapping mind as if
perception slowed to
adrenaline We heard your
music loud and clear, but
where were you?
During peace rallies walking down alleys
Candle vigils for little Ayana who was caught in
crossfire
You profited from our losses
Made enough to buy funeral beds for our babies
Yet drop bombs in our neighborhoods then brag about
it
Careless of collateral damage long as bank accounts
booming
Your crime ridden convictions were cruel crucifixions
You could've least had the decency to attend family
funerals
Carry coffins of once cheerful carcasses
Knock on doors of domestics with blood stained
banners
Dying for flags that didn't need to be fought for
But soldiers sought identity in your creativity
Your hearts must be froze like Ice Cube
But gangsta rap made you do it
And made him do it
And then they do it
Its vicious cycles been spinning wheels
Let that not be your excuse to be excused
Dodging waves returning to murky waters
Brother man let's turn tides

Break generational curses of blind leaders leading
blind leaders
Take trap music,
Straight boot it
Kill switch kill music
If Chief Keef has them marching
Put drill to drill music
Stop thanking God for gun bars we've spread abroad
Bad company corrupts industry
Intent on sales rather than souls
Let's win them back
Bum rush temples
Turn tables of DJs
Crack whips made from mix tapes till it feels like your
wrist breaks
Till Emcees change their messages
Unsatisfied with previous voicemails
Before we blame the system
Before we blame brutality of police
Before we blame the second amendment
Let's strip rapper's writes to bear arms

My Scars

"To share your weakness is to make yourself vulnerable; to make yourself vulnerable is to show your strength." – Criss Jami

Spitology – Objectify

Every poem that i've written, and will continue to write has been more for me than for anyone else. This one, was not one of the hardest to write, but the most uncomfortable to share with you. This poem was, and still is, a deep problem I still struggle with in my heart. Though I have never in my life had struggles with drugs or anything of that such, this problem and its strong hold to me most likely parallel what it feels like to be addicted to drugs. This poem was a serious conversation to myself; to the part of me that just can't let go. Look at it as a letter, a very poetic letter, from the side of me that fights to be liberated from this ill addiction, to the other side that refuses to pull the anchors that are dug into it. The more you keep problems buried in secret, the greater the hold they have unto you. If you find encouragement in this one, that's awesome! If anything, this poem is a reminder of how I can't stop fighting the battle within myself, and at the same time not to put myself under the pressures of my imperfections, because I have a great Father healing my wounds constantly.

"I do not understand what I do. For what I want to do I do not do, but what I hate I do.
And if I do what I do not want to do, I agree that the law is good. As it is, it is no longer I myself who do it, but it is sin living in me. For I know that good itself does not dwell in me, that is, in my sinful nature. For I have the desire to do what is good, but I cannot carry it out. For I do not do the good I want to do, but the evil I do not want to do—this I keep on doing. Now if I do what I do not want to do, it is no longer I who do it, but it is sin living in me that does it." - Paul

Objectify

"This time is the last time", you declare
This addictions additions have multiplied shame
Guilting you into this hedonistic paradox
Chasing highs that fail to make you feel lifted
But only leaves you shaky like Parkinson's
You try to break but just park in sin
Shifting gears back and forth between sober and smashed
But just stall the poison's travel through veins
Swimming through your bloodstream like an egg with tail
Think sex cells
Penetrating the uterus of your mind, paying dearly for its services
Remember sex sells, and it's left you broke for too long
Charged up double A meetings won't energize you with power
This problem's a battery assault, much more fleshy
But today's your last hit before you quit caring
So so long to this addiction with its witty tricks
You'll be running a new engine tomorrow, you say it'll be a quick fix
"This time is the last time", you declare
Caught in deja vu's delusion like wasn't that yesterday's declaration?
But flasks of unfaithfulness got you drunk, drinking and driving
You couldn't help steering stimulating thoughts of her high ways

She was fine like tickets on a freeway
Immoral images intertwining imagination drove your
mind of edge
Oh Susie Q left you so blue, believing her walk and talk
is so true
Teetering of ledges, climbing mountains just to reach
climax
Only to fall from habits you don't think will ever rest
So you rush more idols in your temple, worshipping
lords who warp love to lust
But you cancel out calls from self concern and
conviction
Answering back with texts, like "the overload of
dopamine isn't like smoking dope, I mean
I could be sleeping 'round a circular bed of broads
Chasing tail, thriving for the hunt, but I ain't killing
anybody"
Of course not, you only typed three strikes out in search
bar
And watched the game from comfort of dark dungeon
dorm or dining room
Replaying highlights in your heart, so every beat beats
for more
But God's grace is good, right? He won't mind if you turn
for more
It's been a month and you still stuck in yo sin
You can't even look at ladies the same
Just souls with a bunch of nice parts for purchase
That's why you had them bought and delivered to
bedroom
You no longer notice how wet dreams ironically dried
out your dignity

You ain't no different than a Jack-o-lantern in October
A hallowed head that matches yo heart
But carved with a smile and bright face
So no one would notice your perverse addictions
So strung out on crack, you crack to crocodile tears
Knowing you need help, but so resilient to raising your
hand
You don't want to be looked at like you're stupid
You want to remain the cool kid in class
With first priority eyes that makes male men unwrap
other's gifts
And I know you keep
claiming you got it, and
you're serious Delirious,
God's grace is here to ex
cuses not as excuses
So snap out of this already,
Aubrey!

Spitology – Man Fearing Man

It's funny how i'm writing the story behind this poem this day, after meditating this morning and realizing my nagging need to be relevant. As a faith follower who's been given a mad blessing of an opportunity to have an influence on people that most won't, I am in a part of my journey of not being what Christians tend to make art look like to the world; corny, boring, predictable, awkward, whatever you call it. A lot of what I do honestly is not within churches, youth camps, and youth conferences, but with friends who don't share my convictions. Bars, coffee shops, and soon to be churches who support same sex relations are the places that I share my art. As a person whose art always reflects the gospel in some deep metaphorical way, it's crazy that people who don't share my same convictions love and honor my work. To me, the biggest challenge with this is remaining myself; The authentic, loving, risky, awkward individual that God has made me to be. Not feeling a need to give up who I am to anyone; whether that be someone who believes God is a phony, or the Christian who believes that I should be more obvious and loud with my convictions. I have been in both places, and they are both super uncomfortable on a soul level. For me, it came from a deep place of fear and pride. I once feared the day someone called me out or even got angry due to my belief in God, and on the other end I was fearful of someone on the Christian side judging me because of my love for coffee stout beer. When it came to pride, I loved hearing people snap and be in awe of my abilities, not my faith, while on the other side people praised my attitude of not seeing barriers and going to the 'unsaved' (for the record, I don't take a liking to that phrase) and sharing my faith driven art. Both sides were pulling me into places that weren't me. Because I knew that if I were to just be me, someone on each side would grow suspicious of me. This though, is the uncomfortable road many world changers traveled. Martin Luther King, Mother Teresa, Jesus. Not saying that I will be a world changer like them, but in their journeys, they faced great adversity on both sides and accepted this even if it took them to the grave.

My biggest advice I give to anyone whenever I talk to them is to be authentically them. The 'them' that God purposed them to be. It may look weird and different to people, but let them deal with it. I am still learning to not let fear and pride control who I truly am.

"I yam what I yam" - Ralph Ellison (The Invisible Man)

Man Fearing Man

My efforts to stay relevant make me irrelevant, and
irreverent
I desire to please you all too much
Much more than I yearn to speak truth
Putting emphasis on my creativity
Marrying metaphors and similes
Rhyme schemes and alliterations
And wordplay?
Incredible!
Speaking parables to pair a bull's
Eye with another aiming to be lovers
Find an ark and part to paradise without pay
'Cause I know a guy
I will make all these cool mentions
And not mention my convictions
Hit button and abort mission
Of telling you about a homeless rabbi who suffered
under crucifixion
Providing a drive that you and crew should fix on
But I conceal truth like a criminal
Instead go subliminal
Being more conscious and philosophic
Without mentioning name of the Son of my Father
And I could make up any excuse
Like I don't want to offend
Religion is dead
Or I don't want to be written off like a check
But if i'm brutally honest
It's because I fear your opinion

Cousin of Peter
Bold with brothers and sisters who be believin'
But deny Christ 'round heathens
Unready when they keep asking
No defense when they're attacking
Unwilling to suffer name callings that hit like whips and lashings
I'm a slave to your words
Prisoner to your thoughts
So worried about offending you
Sitting in on your coffee break gossip
As you joke about how fat our boss is
Or how good looking his wife is
I join in with giggles and banter
Knowing that this kind of calling out ain't the answer
But i'd rather be down than to stand up
I just value your opinions too much
In love with your praise that raise my pride and ego
More than the Man who died for me
Took my sin and chose to veto
And wants this deal to be heard by every ear
But your reaction to this truth is what I fear
To be honest
It's a reflection of my love for self
Not wanting the image of me to become weak in your head
Not ready to take thorns to head instead of rose petals tossed at feet
Reluctant to taking up a cross carved with rumors and gossip in it
Going from Aubs. the brilliant to Aubs. the bigot

Saying "Jesus" under my breathe when professed in
poetry
To stay in safe from name bashing and brutality
To remain in all normality
Sink back to mediocrity
As long as you'll applaud for me
What's wrong with me?
I should care less what you think of me
Call me Jesus freak
Bible geek
Say I stink, but
I should turn cheek
It's been written in stone that He was despised so you'll
no doubt hate me
But i'll love you no matter how mad I make you
When I say Jesus came to save you
Not out of religious duty
But out of revealing relationship fully
So for now
I'm here to entertain
Make you laugh, snap, gasp
While also letting you know there is a life for you that
everlasts

Spitology - Love Cuts Deep

When I was twenty-five, I faced the worst physical, mental, emotional, and physical pain that I had ever experienced in my life. An experience that gave me a first-hand perspective of how Jesus felt when he knew the kiss of Judas was not of commitment, but betrayal. For the sake of honoring the people involved, I don't want to expand on how I was betrayed. Just believe me when I say that it hurt me deeply, much more than I ever thought I could be hurt. I cried, I was angry, I contemplated suicide, I questioned all those around me who claimed to be my friends. I was at a massive low point, and it felt far from good. Even with all this considered, I can honestly say that I clung onto God harder than I ever have; praying that through this season I was in, I would not all hatred, violence or revenge rule in my heart. I prayed that God would be there to comfort me in my honest lamenting, expression of emotions and not allow me to soak in a tub of bitterness. People will say it's wishful thinking and dishonesty with yourself, but I truly believe that from this experience, it is totally possible to love those who purposefully stab you in the back. You don't have to hang out with them as if nothing happened, or even associate with them anymore, but it is possible to still

love those people. This betrayal that I faced pushed
me into stepping outside of myself into a
shadowy place. I had to leave my rights, leave my
entitlements, and just be in the arms
of God and just shed myself. Cry, yell, whatever I had to
do in order to find that Greater
Spiritual Peace that transcends all worldly logic and
pain. It was in that place, God showed me how to truly
loves those who do wrong against me.

"There are only really a few stories to tell in the end,
and betrayal and the failure of love is one of those good
stories to tell." - Sean Lennon

"Most of all, love each other as if your life depended on
it. Love makes up for practically anything." – Paul

Love Cuts Deep

Laymen say that you healed lame men
That your shoulders are an ocean for me to cast anchor
of care upon
And your arms are strongholds for the weak
And your hunger for righteousness is what drove you t
swallow death
And that you're a giant handkerchief over earth
Erasing tears from every eye
Wiping disgracing from every shunned face
They say if I seek I find
Well i've been searching
With stab wounds from backstabs
Heart ripped, trust stripped
Severely bleeding beyond imagine
Imagining your personhood before me
As I crawl
Clawing concrete to reach your dragging robe
Telling myself if I only brush fingers against its canvas
It would fix this portrait
Stop breaks on this joy ride
No, train of chaos whose tracks trail to hell
Where legions of demons drown me
Smothering my flame as fleeting feet march
Making suicide sound like the sweetest release from
teeth of beasts
Somedays suffering substitutes slumber
Rewinding scenes of unseen betrayal
And its replay value won't minimize
But I refuse to let face depict devastation in heart

With a smile that beams with life
While what's hidden in darkest caverns shrieks "kill me!"
This death that riots peace
protesting in mind is too much to
handle I'm Wile E. Coyote crushed
under a thousand tons of torment
I'm crushed! Save me!
From internal and external voices enticing me to hate
Detest humans who heap hot coals unto my head
Though bandages of apologies and sorrys sooth for a moment
The sword's stabbing pain still leaves me paralyzed
No matter what
Remind me of your love for the knife wielder
For they knew not what they did
Didn't realize their pursuit of pleasure would drive pain
Would cause mind to black out as havoc wreaks
Waking up to surrounding cities shattering and shaken
By earthquakes under post traumatic stress disorder
Cracking under pressure with every flashback
While every step under public eye tears of anxiety
As fellows line up to lash stones at a sinner who expects
nothing short of an ugly execution
When every night belly buries itself in bottomless pit of pills
Till numb from numbness
Till sleeps so favored for its correlation to death
For blood stained
hands deserved to
be damned And
God's grace has all

rights to turn away
Satan's shackles are
just too loud!
Jangling across floorboards whose creak belittles
Shamefully dragging down soul train line of gavel
wielding worshippers
Shouting names that would never be
screamed in sanctuaries Saints
tongues turn to satan's swords
Save them savior! They know not what they do!
Laymen say your love is a rainfall in scorching heat
Descending over the abused and the abuser
The used and the user
You turn our mess into a message
Testifying of your sweet deliverance
Save us and shame the devil deviating us from your
dominion
Run his raiders into swine spilling them into the sea
Pull our eyes to Calvary's beautiful sacrificial
monument
Where blood and water poured from ribs to cover and
cleanse us
From our fatal fall so short of your glory
Guiltiness that sat on throne of our blood stained palms
has perished
Death's prick diminished like aging columns
Leaving life to be the only pillar to stand on
Our scars may cripple
But your comfort carries us
Hell may knick our souls
But your love cuts deep

Spitology – Understand

Early this year, I almost lost a relative very close to me to an attempt of suicide. I feel convicted even as I type this out, because I have yet to share this poem with this relative. Just know, by the time it has reached your eyes, it will have reached his first. This relative, though very close, has never been told by me how meaningful his life is. If he would've died from the suicide attempt, I would've been cursed with words that remained unsaid, actions that remained undone, and relationship that remained shallow. Before this event, I contemplated suicide in 2016 after a very hard season of my life. From relationship issues, to financial fears, I felt like life just wasn't worth the pain. It sucks to put this out there, especially since I know better. But the world's hand of pressure will always push out logic. The world will constantly tell you that you're not enough, will remind you of the lie of security, and will scream out your failures daily. And it will hurt you bad. This is where the soul meets its shaping tool. What the world uses to break you, God uses to shape you. It won't make sense, but we can't deny that if we give up persevering independently and lean on the people around us, the end of certain seasons condition us to be stronger for those to come. So, this is for you; you who feels the pressures building up around, squeezing you to the point of giving up. Understand that I understand. And this poem isn't much, but I hope an embrace of a loving friend is felt.

Understand

Understand that I understand
Somedays it feels we're here to suffer
Like the universe has beef with us
And is pressuring us to tap out
Every step forward is on a treadmill
So it's like we really don't make and advancements
Just enough movement to keep above surface
Continuously kicking for if we stop we sink
And sometimes that seems better than fighting for breath
I understand
That water pressure pressed my chest countless times
After being cheated on by my fiancé
Faith felt like it went with wind
Leaving me to be cold and alone
Like standing in the eye of Antarctica
Bare footed and stripped body
Placed trust in nobody
But still needing somebody
Maybe i'll find that when I leave body
Behind like a pilot ejecting from cockpit of plane before pulverized
But I realized who I gave controls over too
And that this broken jet still has gas in its tank
Thank the Captain who cruised contemplations in different direction
Because i'm still alive
But understand that I understand

Somedays it feels like we're here to suffer
Like the universe has beef with us
And is pressuring us to tap out
The U.S. lacks compassion for us, how ironic
We've been walled in way before Trump
Bills, rent, loans, and credit stacked around us
If this brings anxiety, no worries
There are counselors and facilities for that
So take hold of those bricks to add them to the
Bills, rent, loans, and credit stacked around you
Until there's no place to look but up
And we're so down by depression death sounds like a
deal we can't dodge
But that devil is a liar
Look for the ladder loosed from above
Up is the answer
Just not through the nudge of suicidal shoves
I know it seems so easy and accessible
Like that drink of antifreeze
Will stop suffering cold in its tracks
But there's an alternate curing concoction
That doesn't involve toxin
And it's been embedded in you since day one from God's
son
It's called Grace
But understand that I understand
Somedays it's easier to remain down than stand
That voice of vice seems viciously victorious
And songs of sorrow seem like the best counselors
But every road to suffering ends shortly
Every "no" to suicide's "yes" is a loss he must digest

Every will to live is a starkly extended middle finger to satan
And every weeping eye will be wiped by Joy's hand
Dark nights evaporate to Son's arrival
I'd be lying if I said I understood the why
Why houses must fall before being built back up
Why the world wars so hard against us
But understand what i've grown to understand
That suffering hung even Earth's greatest One
Even he rose above the sting of the evil one
Your beautiful wrists don't have to wear scars
Your beautiful neck needs no adornment of rope
This world will press you until you can't cope
But then rises a Spirit that impresses hope
Understand that great bad brings greater good
Lifting tears muscle tissue but builds bigger muscle to take on more
Understand that
Though you feel like you're less
You're made for more

Spitology – The Interview

Once upon a time I was engaged to someone who was obviously not the one for me. Everyone around me noticed this but me, and let me know during my engagement (only ride or die homies do that). As I look back at it now, I am truly seeing how subjective I was in that season. I remember one conversation I was having with my good friend and brother one day after I proposed to this person. Obviously seeing what I didn't at the time, he was telling me how he was engaged once before he met his wife. As he was ending this story, he told me something that just spoke volumes to me; "being engaged is an interview process man. Just because they have a ring or a new title doesn't mean they made it into the office." Though this conversation wasn't the turnaround of my decision, it was one that I deeply resonated with after I broke our engagement. We were both being madly immature in our relationship. Our values would always clash; I valued not sleeping in the same bed together, she did not. She valued starting a family and dropping all of our individual aspirations in a blink of an eye, I thought that was absurd (and still do). The list goes on. But the thing is even with all these contrasts we had, we still attempted to squeeze each other into the other's values, and were trying to mask how miserable we really were. We were settling. It was nothing short of God's plan that we didn't end up being together. Though there was great heartbreak, great wisdom and discernment was drawn from this experience. If I could sum it up in one word, it would be this: wait. We

hear it all the time, but for those who don't mind the repetitive lessons
we so often need, don't be so dang quick to search for someone to be with. Be honest with yourself if you really love the person you're with; do you really not mind their unhealthy habits? Do you love them or just love the idea of being in love with them? Being engaged is like an interview for a job, and when you accept that position at the altar, you're in that career for life brother man (.. Or, sister woman?). Don't be that statistic of people who resign if they aren't happy with their 'job' after a few months or years. Love shouldn't be all heady, but to give your whole entire being to a person is something that shouldn't be just tossed to the first person who fills out an application to your heart.

"Don't awaken love, don't arouse love, until I am ready"

The Interview

A friend once told me
Being engaged is an interview process
We've all experienced our first interview
And the following preparations
Trimming hairs from head
For cleanliness cuts deals
Press iron to slacks, shirt, and shine shoes
Wash face of former days' dirt
Brush teeth bearing last week's brownies
Practice enunciating every adjective accurately
And shake hands with selves
To judge whether it's professional enough
For the fine female or marvelous man
Whose presence imitates that of an overseer
As we grow anxious over dinner table duplicating
desktop
Digesting questions
Regurgitating dressed up responses
Layout resume wrung of wrongs
Putting our best up front to not get turned down
Palms profusely permeating sweat
Choking on words that'd seize success
Sharing stories of struggle under stress
Bearing uncertainties that weigh down our chest
For we don't know if we should stay or go
Gain job this day, or be faced with a "no"
Yet worries fleet when we're accepted in the ring
Boxing any ambiguous voices that may challenge us
Accepting job with joy
Basking in accolades from fam and friends

Who say we've finally made it
Feeling grown up
Changing that Facebook status from single to
Employed
Employing skills and talents to tackle responsibilities
Toiling towards employee of the month status
To boast a bit more
Passionately putting persona to perilous death
Just to feel like you're living
Ignore feelings revealing that this ain't fulfilling
Doing duties you ain't designed for
Heart hurting from countless office meetings
As you're told of your lack of diligence
How you aren't putting in what the other is putting out
How it feels like you're punching out too early
Yet you're working overtime
Clocked out
Staring outside windows
Wondering if you're really up for this responsibility
Yet you bury uncertainties
Without digging deep
For you know you shouldn't stay
But choose not to go
Remain with job this day
Though insides scream "no!"
Concerned on if it's too late to rethink fate
Palms profusely permeating sweat
Dreams prophesying future regret
Choking on words that need to be voiced
Cease sharing struggles that place you under stress
Afraid of starting over from square one

Petrified of separating something bearing such a great
price
Though cutting deals now saves later
Just because you made the office Jim
Doesn't promise things will work out with pam
Let what I say stick with you
Being engaged is an interview
In its process we shouldn't get so infatuated
That we bear uncertainties
In compartments where they cease to sing
Jail birds whose tune turns trajectory toward
discernment
So before vocal chords coarse "I do"
Ask "Do I?"
Do I see chemistry bubble between us?
Do I love her present state, or future image?
Do I avoid caution signs in this fast lane?
These questions called for my answer
Though prone to ignoring phone
And neglect voicemails
They tested me with time
I sat with her in that quiet car for hours
Silent as a study room
Looking to the proctor as a doctor
Praying for an answer to the pain
Forgetting this teacher turns tuneless during test time
Giving me freedom to self grade
Trusting in His text for this open book exam
Marriage is a job with no two week notice
Once you've accept placement
Positions permanent

So divorce mind from divorce
Can you play part?
Or will you just act?
Perform as if everything's alright?
Put on mask for
audience you look to
entertain? This is
more than a play
What God brings together should never be a part
No matter how hard the role is
So when you sit behind that desk on first date
Weigh out retirement plan and pay
Consider the weight
When you're engaged in that ring
Fight your feelings
And ask, "Do I truly accept this position?"
If the answers no
There's still an exit door
And a career
Patiently waiting for your application
Just be okay being unemployed for now

Spitology – Thistles

Doubt; a feeling that we try to avoid at all cost on some many levels. Whether it is continuing to believe that Megan down the street really does have a crush on us, and so it only makes sense to answer the mixture of hormones and bodily brain chemicals that tell us to go to her front step and profess our love to her, though we've never actually talked a day in our lives (spoiler alert: she has a boyfriend and doesn't even know your name), or even deeper than that we doubt that struggle exists. Some of the moments that yielded the best growth were those where I struggled a lot. Whether it was with patience with (junior high) students who refused to shut their mouths while I was attempting to help them with their work, or whether it was stressing about how bills would get paid, the seasons struggling to break free from the thorn bush always bore great scars but great discernment to fall into deeper assurance that God can and will heal those. To me, those moments of pressure sucked, and still do. They feel as if i'm being strangled of all hope, joy, and peace. They truly do, but always promise stronger branches to bloom from branches; growing greater faith, perception, and love for. The thorn bush never wins lest I give into its pressure.

"The seed cast in the weeds is the person who hears the kingdom news, but weeds of worry and illusions about getting more and wanting everything under the sun strangle what was heard, and nothing comes of it." - Jesus

Thistles

Transparency be but a cute comfort word
If we deny being strangled
Doubting doubts we thought long were dead
Had never reincarnated amongst bushes of thorns
With stings worse than its own
With goals to reclaim its throne
As deathly diluted arms wrap around necks
With pressure that could dismember a strong rose from stem
As easy as child's thumb pops off dandelion heads
I've felt this constraint
This trust fall landing
Feeling as if it were within hands holding broken glass
Unapologetically pressing shards to pressure points
Making four phrased words on backs of US dollar bills
Bear no profit
As rent money faithfully gravitates toward collection plates
In my testing of God
Trusting Him to pour plentiful riches from floodgates of Heaven
Just enough to compensate so I don't have to formulate
Excuses for Landlord when Lord lands late blessings
And when His timing and mine don't coincide
My faith that seemed so strong
Gets gag tied
By fear that crept inside
Plundering all my supplies
Persuading me to break engagement with God

Elope from matrimony
And instead be his bride
That's the nature of these adulterous thistles
That rotate hearts like planet Earth
Shifting our face's hemisphere toward darkness
Away from sun that never changes direction
Yet we blame it for burns we've collected
Denounce it due to coldness we've detected
Convinced there's no sun in our solar system
This is the deception of these thistles
The same prickly plant that sarcastically crowned a
King's cranium
Now infiltrates our temple
Wrapping brains like old vines that cling to sides of
sanctuaries
Sending burning sensation to heart
A wildfire reeking of vanity, whose smell is mistaken for
a friendly campfire
Aroma digging anchors within nostrils like hooks that
pierce fish's jaws
Making worldly riches become bait upon fishing lines
Pitching lies that by their strength we're pull from dark
depths
Forgetting whose hand pulled Peter from perilous
plummet
And whose head hung like a wilted flower to advice
from Christ
For selling all his wealth felt like sacrificing every ounce
of good health
Like taking tobacco drags until lungs sagged like eye
bags
Playing tag with throat and cigarette smoke

Till you second hand choke to cancer's stabbing poke
With sharpness that could knick a teen
Making the reach towards Heaven infeasible as
Forcing Joe Camel through cornea of sewing utensil
This is the deception of these thistles
Bent on making your faith a feeble fruit tree
Leaving no leaves for maturation
Our souls are seeds bound to be evergreens
Made to move mountains
Yet satan is a twisted gardener
Looking for ways to tower barb wired bushes above us
With worries he brings
Riches that bling
Pleasures of things
Yet the best things in life aren't things
But the gain found in a King
If we let honesty pry chest cavities
Accept permission to penetrate hearts
We've too often confused pricks of nursing needles with
stabs of poisonous plants
Mistaking God's testing for torment
When pain is the only signal of growth
No path ventured without scrapes and bruises is worth
it
Let's dance in fires of refining
Laugh in face of misery
Endure the thistles
Growing above their reach
Letting lowly learn
And scars teach

Spitology – Deep Dive

I'm a selfish person by nature. To this day, I'm still trying to find balance between a healthy love of self and serving others. I've learned many people have their opinions of selfishness, and I have learned to honor what I learn from them while honoring what my gut says as well. I've noticed personally that I get more selfish the more I worry about my needs and wants. Whether I think about how I need to put in work a certain week pertaining to my art, or whether I ponder my accomplishments that I take so much pride in. All these things pull me back to a shallow reality. I think of living within spiritual awareness and consciousness as being underwater; diving into a vast body of water. As you are diving deeper, all that is shallow and superficial stays floating above surface. I always have to come back to the surface, but when I realize the mystery and beauty of what's below, all that I know above is not as important as it once was. If I deny my soul the dive into that deep secret place where it's just me and God, I grow attached to everything above. This poem was a reminder to me that all things that I have ever earned and will ever earned are great, but they will never give true peace and joy to my soul.

"What is more, I consider everything a loss because of the surpassing worth of knowing Christ Jesus my Lord, for whose sake I have lost all things. I consider them garbage, that I may gain Christ." - Paul

Deep Dive

I could've sworn I drowned this house
Returned rented roof to owner
Who repossessed residence and resident
And sunk it in shallow waters with depth that caused death
This lost city became Atlantic's Atlantis
So that something sacred could substitute
I even hogtied bricks to belongings
And buried them in body of water
Then tossed this body in water
You may call it bonafide suicide
Or a radical irrational action
But it was the sweetest surrender ever experienced
The execute plan was execute man
And rise from river a refurbished remnant
Revived with water wandering within mortal makeup
Divinity dwelling in DNA
Retinas retuned to view valleys in new admiration
See civilians in sights of celebration
Thankful for even the most depraved peoples
More less self so self less was all that was left
But it felt so right
So why has wrong resurfaced?
Trophies, medals, mirrors, me
Coasting surface of sea so suddenly
Reminding me of days dealing dolphins
Profiting piranhas, soliciting sharks for salary
Reminding me of selfish tendencies
How when I saw you, I see food
Put everything at stake on plate

Even if it meant sue she
Long as I ate
Seeing friends as shrimp
Small and insignificant
Frontin' like "Waz up b?!"
While really thinking
"Shh, kay Bob"
Their trust I'd rob so I could eat like a slob
Why do these things show up at the table?
Force feeding my futility that goes down smoothly
Saturation soul with subtle consideration of relocation
So the world could move back move back into center
Circling me like rings of Saturn
Concerned 'bout doing unto me than unto others
Spending money on me over borrowing to broke
brothers
See a means to an end when I stand in front of sisters
If she's sweet like candy I throw her a cane
For my heart becomes a twister
Spreading people out colorfully 'cross my games
For the game I play is twister
The old self was so sinister and seducing
Abusing and using under my doing
If I'm anchored anew in affection
Why doe these things remain my reflection?
Maybe I'm rocking wrong waves
Maybe i'm not supposed to be on any waves
Maybe those items are to hover idly
And this problem's a product of my phobia of falling
deeper

Just maybe that Sovereign Spirit that saved me isn't a
ship
But the sea itself
Making this drownings not short-term but eternal
Calling me from not above but below
Sinking in that secret place
Not looking back at things loosed above
But Beauty i'm bound to find beneath
Shallow self will surf shallow waters endlessly
While descendants descend deep into love
Counting all gains
Mirrors, medals, trophies
Relationships, romance, lusts
Freedom, futility, and trust in own abilities
As a loss compared to the win within
The beginning who began
Where I end

Ponderings

"I think everything in life is art. What you do. How you dress. The way you love someone, and how you talk. Your smile and your personality. What you believe in, and all your dreams. The way you drink your tea. How you decorate your home. Or party. Your grocery list. The food you make. How your writing looks. And the way you feel. Life is art." – Helena Bonham Carter

Spitology – Free Will

The one question that I asked myself that led to this poem, "if Free Will was a person, what would he or she say?" I could be wrong.

"For to be free is not merely to cast off one's chains, but to live in a way that respects and enhances the freedom of others." - Nelson Mandela

Free Will

My name is Will, and I am free
Freeing you from what you deserve, for the nails driven
through His nerves
Served as a full course communion, breaking union of
sin and death
Giving you Myself and Mercy which costed you nothing
The chains have been broken so you know token
His Love that was shown and spoken at the Cross
You've been forgiven, for you knew not what you did
You were subject to judgement, but Jesus became the
topic
Left to bear weight, but God spotted
You from the Heavens and thought
"Since I so love the world, I shall send my one and only
son"
And in turn you received me, Free Will
Because of me, you have life free from consciousness of
transgressions
So you can live in joy, and not die in self-aggression
I am the mercies you breathe in through your nostrils
That first step you take outside your home
That nudge that tilts head up so that pupils connect
With blue skies that reflect in your eyes
I am the reason for your smile and the reason for your
frown
I impel that warm feeling in your heart that starts
When you reminisce on memories that are now afar
I am Free Will, a product of His Will
But as they say, with the good comes the bad
His love, my purpose has inched you out of death

But you run for miles, seeking loopholes in my design
Though you were driven by madness, only receiving a
warning
Because of Christ's initiative of taking the ticket of deat
Buckling you up into safety, you act as my officer
Using me as your get out of jail for free card as you
rebar
And restart in the prison of your pride
I am your cop out when red and blue lights flash within
your temple
Signaling you to avoid the tempter
Who makes wrong turns look right
But you say it's alright, you're only operating under me
Free Will
You use me to back up backlashing
To support drinking habits
To aid immorality that does damage
Broken homes, beat up feelings, hurting hearts
These bring no guilt nor shame
Because the blame goes on me, Free Will
I mean I might as well be called your Nike Shoe
endorser
With the way you 'just do it' without thinking
Because thinking would prompt you to stop and pause
As my voice plays on rewind within canals of your
psyche
Motioning pictures of how foolish it is to flaunt my
freedom
Around on your picket signs as you pick at guys
Who don't say or do what you like
And when you're asked why, I am the One blamed
Free Will

You strap me into the seat of your philosophies
Believing yourself to be a modern day Aristotle
Or Epicurus as you apply me like make-up
To make up foundations to make shady eyes look pretty
You say that because of me, there is no reason to believe
in morality
Because you all are the only beings in this reality
Take gun laws
If you had a friend named Will who carried steel
Because of Free Will, it can be carried anywhere
concealed
Until Will loses a deal to Bill and feels a need to pull the
steal
Then chooses to pop it like pills
And now everyone is sporting my name out white tees
"Free Will"
If I were wings on your backs, you'd all be like Icarus
Flying towards the Sun like a Phoenix
Melting away the true nature of why they're made
As you fall to your soon coming shame
But your persistence
The way rise to party in the USA
I would swear that you all are Jonah's brothers
The way he chose to use free will to follow his "me will"
And was swallowed by Free Will-y
Is no different from the way you try to do things your
way
Instead of trusting The Way
Who paid the way like a toll to save you soul the
expense
So yes, if you have not guessed it by now, Free Will is
not my true name

Just an alias generated by your disconnected thinking
from the Father
I am Grace
Not an idea, but a gift
To give you peace to sit calm like sitcoms are on
Will and Grace
Though you try to cut my series of salvation
And pilot yourself into seasons of rebellion
I will still be Grace, and I will still be free for you
It was His Will to give you Grace
Not as the okay to sin
But to live in Him
I am Grace, and I am free

Spitology – Roxanne

"It's so nice to see a young man reading and writing as opposed to being in front of a piece of technology", this was the compliment given by an old couple at a local coffee shop that ultimately inspired this poem. I sat down with this older couple I met at Coolbeanz. They told me of a story of this woman they knew named "Roxanne". From my understanding, she was a young black woman who wasn't the brightest student academically. Throughout junior high, high school, Roxanne was looked at as a failure by her teachers and peers. Even so, this woman told me that she and a few others heavily invested in her because they saw a great potential within her that went under the radar of everyone else. No matter what the external voices said, they believed that Roxanne had something great to offer this world. Long story short, she ended up graduating a very prestigious university, and taught at a university level as well. This story deeply resonated with me, and just my upbringing as I reflected on it. I am thankful for the many people in my life who believed and saw the better in me. From my Cross Country and Track coaches, my teachers and professors, pastors and friends. There were many times that I felt like a failure because of the way I was perceived by others, but if it wasn't for those people who said "to hell with those lies" and invested in me even when it was hard, I probably wouldn't be writing this book to you. It is amazing how, we can also be that person to others who think lowly of themselves, like Roxanne..

"He was always so zealous and honorable in fulfilling his compact with me, that he made me zealous and honorable in fulfilling mine with him. If he had shown indifference as a master, I have no doubt I should have returned the compliment as a pupil. He gave me no such excuse, and each of us did the other justice." - Charles Dickens

Roxanne

"Have you ever heard of Roxanne?"
An elderly woman inquired of me as we sporadically
broke into conversation
Roxanne was just like me
No so good looking, didn't have much cooking
And though she was under eyes, there were many
overlooking, her
I came to realize that though we never met, Roxanne
and I were twins
Roxanne was like a rock in sand
Buried under society's assumptions
But Roxanne could turn rock to sand, bagging boulders
with strikes of destruction
Disintegrating deductions designed to define her
With a destiny doodled by a Great divine designer
But people prone to obvious greatness wouldn't get this
We all like to believe we're for the underdog
Swinging those with childlike zeal up into
the air of their imagination But do we do
that when we past the broke artist who
works hardest?
Or the 1.6 GPA undergrad whose brain is so weighted
and weary that it under drags? Let's be honest, we
hardly pay homage to those we don't think could ever
bare knowledge
Or maybe we aren't that way at all, doing the hard work
of yard work
Trimming rough hedges that refuse to be hewed
Cutting grass that will only grow back fast

And not even a week in we say, "this yard ain't worth the work"
Preferring an easier task to tackle
But when another worker digs deep into that soil
Planting seeds, fulfilling all needs
Even if it means dirty nails and filthy cut knees
To see desolate grounds bloom beautiful trees
We turn around and say, "I worked that yard, I knew it would grow nice one day"
Don't be mistaken, people aren't projects
But the beauty of brokenness is seeing it fixed
And too often we bail when we see too many fail
So those with rock hard tenacity diminish to sand due to gravity of reality
But when sand is built up to colossal castles we like to take credit in that crafting
I was once that rock turn to sand
But many mentors mended me for they knew God had plan
And they continue to uplift losers to win the stars
Understanding that they were once overlooked
But a King of cosmos continues to overlook
Was pegged like wooden legs to wooden cross where h
overlooked
Observers who viewed him, skewed him, and overlooked him
But he still reverse roles and looked over them
Shifting the repentant from poor to prosperous
Making the blockheads like me cornerstones of community
Though Roxanne didn't look like much to the world

Another tree destined to nothing, sowers sewed threads
of influence to her branches
It's been 'bout a decade since she's seen Roxanne
Never been in the paper for profound progress
Nor interviewed for story, but that's okay
Those who have eyes will see
And those who have ears will listen, as I did that day
Roxanne was one of the meek like me
And those shall inherit the Earth
And outside of it they shall find their worth

Spitology – Vengeance

Now the inspiration from this one came when I was working as a paraeducator for a school in Moline for the mentally and behaviorally impaired. There was a student who went there for behavior, which at times was super hard for me to believe because he was honestly one of the sweetest and most polite students at our school. One you would least expect to have an urge to physically or emotionally harm anyone. Well, one day I was awakened to something I was in disbelief to; this student with a beat red face, angrily struggling with staff who were dragging him down the hallway. Seeing his tearstrickened face and voice that mixed with anger and fear, I remember these words coming out of his mouth, "you're gonna pay for what you did!". Long story short, this student grew angry of another student calling a teacher out of her name. After multiple times of telling him to stop and seeing that fail, he broke down and wanted to physically stop the pain this student was dishing out. As I looked at this student, I was reminded that he was really no different than you and me. When people are doing what we perceive as wrong, and the option of 'being nice' gets rejected multiple times, it seems like our only option is to force them to abide by our rules and regulations. I've seen this with adults who have a heart to mentor young boys by means of forcefully indoctrinating them with what we perceive as 'good'. I've seen this many times in churches when they aim to bend and break people into faith. The vengeful response to brokenness is really out of a good heart, just a wrong approach. It's natural to meet resistance with resistance, but to meet resistance with un-resistance seems illogical and impossible. This student reminded me of this; love and forgiveness is always the overwhelming, transforming force that creates goodness in this world.

"Before you embark on a journey of revenge, dig two graves." - Confucius

Vengeance

And they dragged him by his arms down the school
hallway
Restraining forearms and biceps as if wrestling a
python
The student
Struggling as if a wild beast in chains
Face dim red as if volcanoes exploded through pores
Tears
Running down face
Escaping the monster that his eyes had become
Though teeth were like a lunar eclipse
Grinding over each other upon passage
The son's shine shone through radiation expressed
through vocal chords
"He will pay for what he did"
You see
His Captain Gordon heart met with the signal of his
Batman mind
Convincing him that his motives were that of a hero
Wanting nothing but sweet revenge
Upon foes that murdered feelings of those who modeled
a mother and father in his life
Spilling emotions like blood of robbed bodies in the
alley of anguish
But heart can play a riddler
Playing role of a two-faced joker
Making our most wicked wishes seem like the most
admirable decisions
This student and I

We're no different
The way we bottle up emotions like wine waiting to age
Unmindful that old wine
No matter how good it seems
Will never be perfectly united within the wineskins of
righteousness
We'll always burst out in frustration and spite
You see, our aim is off by a long shot
Believing that showing our guns will ring a
message through the air to our targets But when
has planting bad seeds produced breathtaking
flowers? And how will a sprout born amongst
thorns Learn that it can flourish into a beautiful
lotus?
Brothers, we can't mash morals into youth we mentor
Sisters, we will wake up sleepers when we put
bitterness to bed
Church, a forced faith will push people away from our
indoctrinating death grip
We've made it our obligation to force heaven into
heathens
Neglecting responsibility to love hell out of their bones
We're destined to be Trees of Life
Inspiring roots of evil to leave their soil
Manifesting the true identity of these vagabonds
Passed down from a King whose made them royal
If I learned one thing about this student, it is this
Our hearts will get us carried away
To a place where we mistaken darkness for light of day

Spitology – Tremor

The one thing I love about love is that true love breaks things. True love destroys things. True love tears dow and builds up something new. Whether that be in frien relationships, marriage relationships, and relationship with God. The false, flimsy, and temporary are dismantled. I love it because it's uncomfortable. When was shown my real identity outside of the sphere of influence of the world, I found great love and great struggle with it. My world was falling apart. My view o sex, pride, anger, all these things went through a beautifully painful procedure of remodeling. Though it made me frustrated, though it kept me up at night, though it made me fall to my knees and bawl like a baby, I can truly say I was never harmed in it all. Though I was tossed into a fire that burned away all those things I adopted in my life as truth, I had no burr marks through it all. Change is uncomfortable, and that's why I love it. In this world, we question and run away from the uncomfortable, especially in our Westernized, comfy culture. God shakes things up in our lives, and reveals those things in us that contradic the world's view. And that is okay. That is what love does.

"When you plant something, it must die in the ground before it can live and grow." - Paul

Tremor

You shook my world
From the moment I came to my knees
I needed not to wait for the words "I do"
Because your beauty
To this beast you
Joined in perfect harmony
Reconciling our fallen matrimony
You quaked the ground and entered my city
Your presence
Overwhelming
Towering above skyscrapers
As your monumental majesty scraped up my view
But calling you Godzilla would be rude
Because your beauty is too astounding
And your love was quick to abounding
Into my over-pounding
Butterfly surrounded
Heart
Though we were acquainted only for a few minutes
Love at first sight is not foolishness for you
You were my childhood friend
Much sweeter than any girl next door
You knew me before I knew me
Crafting the master plan to make me your man
Though I was a grouch like Oscar, living in my filth-
filled atmosphere
And that's what drew me
I was old bones dead and broke
But your benevolent breath blew

And constructed a new me
The lithosphere of my being cracked and fell apart in
your presence
But your hands pieced new tectonic plates
In its place
Unveiling your beautiful gleam that now shines through
this face that is smiling
I had to know you
I wanted to know you
Not like I did in the past
Passively proclaiming.to know you
When I was just a slacker
Sitting slothfully in back of Spanish class
I only conocer'd you
But now I want to know you passed the text in the book
and facts
I yearn to saber you
Though you continually wreck my blueprints
Scatter my belongings like plaid
But you're only destroying synthetic elements
Periodically building new tables that were stable
Your breaking isn't bad
Every building that collapsed
Was reconstructed to a better function
And somehow in all this destruction
I was left unscratched
Your Grace amazed me
And I just can't fathom how at one time could not need
you
I thought I didn't need you
To me you were just an ex
And while others say you never existed

But we weren't ready to pursue true love
We never really risked it
Now I can't go a day without thinking of you
Keeping your cross in mind
Keeps you crossing my mind
Like the well planned and thought out nomination of
the gadget for show and tell on Friday
I just have to show You to others
My friends think i'm crazy
That i'm out of my mind and greatly conceited
But they aren't alone
I'm regarded as an irrational radical lover because of
your name
As well as your other lovers
They say we should keep our relationship private like
parts veiled by pants
In fear that when revealed, we'll be put to shame by how
small it really is
No one yearns to be your bride
You're like the neglected groom
Left at the alter
And i'm guilty of stealing your Grace and leaving like a
robber
But you never faltered
You're a reckless-zealous leader
Whose presence is like ether
Smelling sweeter than perfume
Containing a fire that's ready to go boom
Wrecking everything before you that took up room
Like a child without his Ritalin
Placed in a house full of vases after given five hour
energy and sugar

breaking and scattering everything like reeses pieces
But cleans up the broken pieces
And replaces them with nicer pieces
And from there the homeowner's joy increases
The factor that fractures many
That shook the core of my being
Is the fact that a relationship with you means to empty
Ourselves like pockets after Black Friday
That's a sacrifice that others can't pay
Because they want it their way
So they boot you to the highway
Without saying "have a nice day"
A relationship with you means danger
But an exchanger
Changing and rearranging our hearts and minds
To a better design
To something eternally divine
But we must de-vine and resign
Then re-sign to the true Vine
So I make you mine
Becoming a free man from slavery
But enslaving myself to your freedom
You ask for a lot but a little
But a lot because you paid a lot for us
You have a reputation of shaking worlds
Your presence is intimidating
Maybe that's why many choose to stay away from you
Because with you comes tremors that shake and break
Revealing in us what's real and what's fake

But takes the fake and gives
us something worth
keepsake A relationship.
Better than any happily
ever after ending story
Because your glory is
happily everlasting after
we end Ourselves.
Putting our pride on the shelf
Trading it for your instrument of death for our
shoulders
Giving us a love that can move boulders
It is true that you wreck everything in your path
But after the debris settles
Your wonderful hands lead us to a love that
Everlasts

Spitology – Briar Rose

.

Where this poem came from... I will be completely honest with you. I was at a bar called RIDRS with a friend. It's like a country club type bar; full of country music, line dance, and my personal favorite, swing dancing! As I was sitting down having conversation with a friend, a woman a little older than myself at the time accidently spilled her beer on me. She was under the influence, so I didn't trip. In her state of mind at the moment, she thought it'd be fitting to "apologize" by raising her shirt up (bra still all there...) at me. Yeah, it made the rest of the time awkward there. People who saw this in the surrounding area were laughing, but I am honest when I say that I was deeply bothered. I don count myself traditional or old school in any sense of those phrases, but one thing that I have learned to honor, for both men and women, is the philosophy purity. With that said, I was a woman user when I was in high school and freshmen year of college; sexually active due to the external pressure of culture that care not about this foreign, archaic value of purity; waiting until marriage to be closely intimate with your significant other. It wasn't until I was twenty-five that I realized the fullness of why this is a thing. It was much more than religious or pious practice to me, because most of the time that rhetoric is super shallow, rule-based, and ironically misogynistic. It was a deep spiritual and emotional understanding of how sex is vulnerable, the body and its revealing is vulnerable, and should be shared only with that person who has committed to a covenant of vulnerability with us. Ther

126

are so many sleeping beauties in this world, men and women, slumbering from this sacred truth due to a culture that has been long distracted and rooted in the lies of sex being a thing that people should just naturally do. I believe that with that grew a lack of self dignity, self respect, and in and of that respect for others. As I pondered this, I thought about the story "Sleeping Beauty", hence its original name, "Briar Rose".

"There's more to sex than mere skin on skin. Sex is as much spiritual mystery as physical fact. As written in Scripture, 'The two become one.'
...Or didn't you realize that your body is a sacred place, the place of the Holy Spirit?"- Paul

Briar Rose

You should have never gave pupils permission of
passage
Never allowed eyes to take gaze of your garden
Stuck was my body as if
branches of briar bond
biceps Constricting
core with wrath of a
protective Father Did
you know you killed
me that night?
But I wonder how many other princes hang deceased
within these woods?
Have caught wind of your sacredness only to get
cursed?
Condemned with corneas that cry to be chopped out
and tossed to flames
For they know of the holiness they should've never
beheld
That day my heart cried for you
For we usually project what we ourselves wrecked
And my dear, you have put to sleep a solemn virtue
Have been pricked by spindle that spin sackcloth that
covers your head
You have been blinded to beauty you've borrowed
Strong drink made you unable to think
But drunken spirits always reveal sober scars
And darling
Covering cuts with alcohol always wind up burning us
after

Your body's a temple
A castle guarded by giant hedges withholding your
holiness for Him
Not all of them
But once you've allow vagabonds to break past
vineyards
It's easy to turn temples to welcome inns
Where you welcome in any individual that depicts a
prince
Putting frame on display for fellows to see or feel
Though you're a masterpiece not meant to be touched
With plenty of finger prints across your sleeping body
Many impure puckers place on slumbered lips
This what happens when love arises prematurely from
playpen
Crying from crib in vexation
Irritation to no one concerned of its signaling cry
That whistles through radio
For the only focus is to find a fellow that makes us feel
less lonely
These innocent intentions always twist like the thorn
bush
That were never meant to make murder of males minds
Not to blame shift, 'cause the thing is
Princes put nobility on shelfs
Act as animals in the Serengeti
Grab machete
And cut down women's walls with wicked words
That wear warm welcoming rhetoric that sounds like
the sweetest chivalry
Including me
The prince and predator in me are always at it

One fighting for nobility
While other wants to use charming abilities
To design deceiving dashing dignity
To take over with tyranny
All your sense of purity
Dear, you're body is a temple
A sanctuary surrounded by briars shielding your
sleeping beauty
Don't despise or deny their defense
Believing that you are something less
Thinking your sacredness is too selfish to hold to
esteem in society
Though fairy tales are often frail
There's a prince who will be allowed passage passed
those thistles
Unscaved by spikes, gentle to that garden guarding your
Heart
Walking through woods with wise worry
Unwilling to step on any cracks and crevices of your
core
Climbing your castle with caution
Gazing your gorgeous glimmering face as if it's a sun
setting the serengeti
Stunned, humbled in disbelief of disposition
To him, laying his unworthy lips upon yours will wreck
him
Shake the foundations of his skeleton
Cause heart to hold breathe in
bottomless brooks of euphoria
Do you know you will kill him
that day?
Yet make him feel so alive

As he will you
Hundreds of years may pass till his presence is present
But remember you're a gift
Boxed and bowed in blessing
So special that unwrapping yourself would
Spoil unworthy infants
Your body's a temple
Never let layman lay them eyes upon your inner courts
Looks kill

Spitology – Gospel

One thing I overemphasize about myself is that I am anti-corny. When it comes to how I do art, I put my whole mind, heart, body, and soul into creating something different and unpredictable every time. As a Christian, if I claim to believe in a God whose creativity is out of this world, there's no reason why I should not reflect that poetic creativity myself. With that said, and I say this in all honesty, a lot of the times that I hear the Gospel presented through art is mad corny; the presentation, corny. The lyrics, corny. The instrumentation and all, corny. I don't know why it is, but religious folks have a hard time tapping into that deep creative sphere of our minds. Yet, I also came to a humbling truth at the end of writing this one too; that sometimes 'corniness' can't be helped, and when it happens, we should embrace it. So this poem is my attempt of describing what the Gospel looks like from my poetic perspective.

Gospel

"He gave his life for me"
Such a well known Christian Cliché
But do we really know what he had to pay?
As lip synced songs loosely leave lips
While arms
Raise high as if
submitting all authority
to a robber Do we truly
understand our
surrender?
Sunday morning
The time of day we feel obligated to
Sit with backs against pews pleasantly
Following teachings with a semester like short term
memory
That fails and drops out between our seat and exit door
Yet we walk in the stride of a university graduate
Meditating on time sacrificed
Sat still
Fighting fatigue
Tossing up caps in celebration of our good deed for the
year
Though we enter into the real world unequipped
Mind numb to the implications of salvation
Hearts cold to conviction that cries for our conversion
Unwilling to love our neighbors
Unrelenting to letting ourselves be sold out
Rooting ourselves in self fulfillment

Rather than the soil that a sacred seed split himself for us
Saplings to find solitude
Lifting the blade from our branches
For he joyfully chose to take those scars
Shred red
Beat blue
To white out wrongs within world
Proclaiming to be the way, truth, life
Though they claimed this Jew lie
He rose before the fourth
Though Gethsemane heard cries that were unheeded
Saw pores bleeded while he pleaded
"Father, take this mission from me if it isn't needed"
And all his friends retreated
While critics deemed him a demon
He carried his cross with perseverance
With an endurance that endure rants
Yet we settle for being indoor ants
Crawling in underneath nice ceilings
Digesting sermons only if they stimulate our feelers
Ignorant to the fact that God could've crushed us
But pressed the weight of His love upon our hard hearted exterior
So His hugs and kisses could XO skeletons
It only makes sense to exchange our gain
For a prophet that profits all
And the biggest offense is to passively acknowledge such a gift
He's the resurrected King
The reassurance that Life
Will be erected within vessels

Prone to deadly things
Yes, he's the resurrected King
Who desires to resurrect you and me
Not just yearly, nor weekly
But daily

Spitology – Wasted Words

Have you ever heard of Dr. Masaru Emoto? He was a researcher from Japan whose known for his study that led him to making a profound connection between water molecules and human consciousness. He conducted an experiment where he exposed water to different sounds, pictures, and words; then he would freeze these water molecules. As a result, the water exposed to positive words, pictures, and vibes crystallized into beautiful patterns. As for the ones that were exposed to the negative? They formed into distorted, less elegant shapes. There are many things that you can connect this too when it comes to us humans, whose makeup is mostly water, and what we take in visually or audibly. The biggest takeaway I got from this experiment was that words have power to build beauty and distort something that was made for more. The words we tell ourselves, or receive from others, or dish out to people have the strongest advantage to create greater positive consciousness or negative ponderings. With how precious words are, it always convicts me how much I waste them on a daily basis, in both nonsense and length. A few words have greater power than an essay of carefully examined criticisms.

"Words from the mouth of the wise are gracious, but fools are consumed by their own lips." - Author of the book of Ecclesiastes

Wasted Words

I've wasted words
Left words wickedly wasted without warning
To hearts, they brought burning
Made insecurities start churning
Faces of confidence started turning
Spirits discouraged started yearning, for life
Because this tongue cut like a knife
It's like a lethal scalpel, I blame it on Adam's apple
It's stuck in my Adam's apple, that there is the prime
example
I pushed blame on a fruit that inspired Snapple
Wasting words trying to defend my babel
Others are sickened 'cause my breath is kickin'
Like Spartan 300 and Bruce Lee kickin'
People's passions and personalities into prisons
Leaving them down casted, instead of uplifted
I'm a man of unclean lips, among people of unclean lips
Every word we say is from the pit, poison in every
syllable we spit
Dirty mouths like fallen comets, gums in need of Orbit
But that's not it, the mouth of this wannabe rev runs
Lips dressed in a tracksuit and Adidas
Working words out, but when it walks this way
Dull points are crafted like a bad arrow smith
Bowing tongue shoots carelessly into the air
Making foolish words hard to bear
Folly filled phrases fill the numerator
Outweighing the wisdom of the denominator
So my improper words are improper fractions
Saying things out of pride just for a simple reaction

Hoping to win some attraction, fan-based interaction
But if I sell out wisdom just to be heard
That's a bad transaction
Let's put God into the equation
The Trinity whose infinity like beyond
Compared to us, the zeros
If He remains the dividend, we will never end
But if we switch our roles from the divisor
We will be nothing but an ear and eye sore
The words of the foolish are many, so the mouth speak
nonsense by the plenty
But on that day in Acts 2, the spirit descended like fire
Touched lips like the hot coal that made Isaiah inspire
And flipped Peter's speech to a different tone
As disciples acquired new language without Rosetta
Stone
Words will never be the same
We have the breath of a dragon
Not full of senseless drag-on, but passion to pass on
Our bellies that were once dormant volcanoes
awakened
Bringing forth the same flame that Jeremiah couldn't
contain
Consuming listening hearts like a wildfire
With no intentions of bringing down, but lifting souls
higher
Just as a small fire flickering amongst twigs can build
the biggest flames
A statement of love can crack open eyes to the heavens
above
Such an influence can't be of our own merit

But a power that manifests from our reliance on the
Spirit
The power of life and death lie behind these teeth
May others feel the warmth of Christ's love
And not be burnt by words from hell's heat
That would be wasting words

Spitology – Ambidextrous

It surprises people when I tell them what first influenced my poetry. Because though poetry obviously sparked inspiration, it was greatly built upon by other different arts. Hip hop and battle rap were the biggest game changers when it came to how I thought about art, how I wrote, and how I performed. These mediums created the many unique elements that I add to poetry now. Some people love it, and some people are questionable of it, which is great. The day every single person loves what you do, is the day everyone has become robots. The thing I love most about art is that it can challenge your worldview if you let it. Not in a way of rejecting every single thing you know and believe, but to question every aspect of what you believe and to ask yourself why you believe it. Apart from the message in art, the style of music can do that as well. My freshmen year of college in Fort Dodge made me question myself as to why I hated country music so much, and in turn led me to realize I really didn't have a reason for the dislike. Now I listen to country whenever I have the chance, and that in turn led to my love for swing dancing! Difference is beautiful, and to me is just a metaphor of God's vast creativity that isn't just contingent on pious things; church, 'churchy' music, poetry, paintings. If we put our biases on shelf for just a few minutes and see things as they are, and let them be what they are, we see the great and amazing uniqueness in them. To me, that's true worship.

Ambidextrous

You'll love one
Hate the other
Maybe you have admiration for both
Regardless of stance
These fellows are brothers
Like Abel and Cain
Ones accepted while the ones rejected
Neglected like a person virally infected
Injected with instrumentals
And this makes people judgmental
One is straight to pencil tip point
Poised in properly perpetuating passion
Reaching past your rib cage to caress corazon
With compassionate composition changing your
disposition
Number 2's does the same
With 808s boom bap behind pain
Making you groove
Making you dance
Canceling cares of whatever your circumstance
Ones adored
The other abhorred
One holds history of black liberation
As is the other
But brings folks ears to frustration
One has eloquence
The others known to spark violence
One makes tears nudge
The other gets judged

Regardless of difference
I love both
And as long as these lips move
You'll hear my sons in same room
Descending from diving board tongue
Making a splash sprinkling all bystanders
Without warning
You'll love me
And hate me
Either way
You'll leave the party under influence
Tipsy off inspiration and drunk off offense in the same
day
Because of me
Sorry but not sorry
This ain't cookie cutter artistry
You'll take every fiber of me
You can't see the Langston Hughes and Gil Scot Heron in
me
While bypassing Kanye, Outkast, who influenced me
You have better chance driving down south
Avoiding eyes from seeing Waffle House signs
You can't judge books by beats brother
Nor deem dialect by delivery sister
These two outage all of us
Lived through cotton picking
Great depression living
Survived East Coast, West Coast Rivalry
They have stories to be told
Ones that deserve our ears attention
So leave preconceived notions at door

Hear the heart behind tone
Don't retreat out of legalistic ignorance
But test this with souls open to the Spirit, and don't wine
There's a message bottled in seas of similes, metaphors, and imagery
From church steeples, and Farmer's Markets full of peoples
Wedding Sanctuaries and front desks of your secretary
Poetry and Hip Hop will wrestle you till your hip pops
Give you hot feet, bring flip flops
Provoking thought like poking lions with tree limbs till heart stops
Regardless of the stance of many I'll forever be the Metaphysical lyrical individual
Pivotal never pitiful
Very so analytical
Always spitting the spiritual
'bout a Man who made miracles
Open mics, and through stereo
Consider me
Oh so ambidextrous

Spitology – Tell 'Em

This poem honestly had no rhyme or reason, but was the product of a writing challenge my good friend and brother Chris dished out to the poetry team he leads. It's an echo to Carven Lissaint's "Tell Them" poem; speaking on all the things he would want people to know about himself when he's passed away. So this challenge for me was to think about what would I want to leave here for people in the least words that I can if I were to be gone tomorrow. It turned out to be a pretty dope piece, to me!

"Why, you do not even know what will happen tomorrow. What is your life? You are a mist that appears for a little while and then vanishes." - James

Tell 'Em

Tell 'em I died way before grave grabbed me
Way before casket closed around corpse
Way before cancer that put me to bed
Or the shot that penetrated this martyr's head
Though dead tell them i'll be more alive than i've ever been
Tell morticians to burn my body to ashes
And dash them over the Mississippi
That river that witnessed my maturation
Consumed sweat of summer's sweltering sunshine
From college days when Cross Country training
Took me on long runs on bike path by waterways
And caught tears of countless cold nights
When eyes would gaze across
Loss for words would wrap 'round lips
And heart would feel solemn from this sea's sound of bliss
As winds blew kiss 'cross its murky waters
Creating a soundtrack of love
That made city lights shine a bit brighter
Those waters were my sanctuary of worship
Tell onlookers that look on over my obituary
That I saw through death's intimidation
And didn't deem him scary
Though he speared me
Hoping sharpness pierced me
It's sting rendered worthless
Extend my thumb and index finger in mockery
To his failed robbery
Tell them my American horror stories

145

That transparency within inadequacies
Days during Rock Island High School
Sophomore, wise fool
Fit in to be cool
Cold heart, whirlpool
Creating conflicting tides to hide shame
Brutally beat bullies bloodily
Just to gain fame
Grasped gun with gorilla grip
Thank God I never aimed
Stole purity of princesses
'Cause that's the game guys played
I'm so ashamed
Tell them i'm sorry
The women I abused
The bullies I bruised
The friends I used
Tell them i'm sorry
Tell them I found redemption
When I deserved a chastising lesson
That pocketbook Bible
That I only cracked opened when opportune
Retuned signals in psyche
Seeing scripture from different picture
Perspective
And wasn't within walls of worship halls for it to be
effective
Tell them I found forgiveness
Which transformed the heart of this unworthy worthy
witness
I haven't been the same since this

Tell them perfect wasn't my expertise
I still struggled severely
Took walls down fearfully
Sinned so severely
Though I received love in emotionless manner
Every act of admiration seared me sincerely
Tell them I was thankful
For every brother who believed in me
Every sister who grieved with me
Parents, pastors, passerbyers
Who unlocked the best in me
They were all proof of God's Grace and divinity
Tell them I was never afraid to go against grain
Never believed what Western Church clergy said
Just because they had a degree they gained
Though I held convictions with strong apologetics
I'd ditched them in seconds to show outsider's affection
God gave me passion and purpose through poetry
Prolific efficiency was but a dim glimmer of God's
creativity
Tell them I wasn't afraid to be me
Saw no need to please pious people
Appease church folks for praise
But ironically found home amongst homies
Who avoided church for days
I pray that I shone a ray
Tell them I found peace
Tell them I never reached a destination
But journeyed joyfully
Tell them this world hurt me like hell
Tell them I loved like Heaven

Tell them I was never a reverend
But in Love I found true reverence
Tell them I didn't regret my past
Because God's presence
Tell them though I lived
Death was an everyday duty
So this grave that got me
I was prepared for its embrace
The moment I let go of my life long before
Tell them I died ready

Spitology – Bell Ringer

I am deeply convicted as I remember why I wrote this poem. We all grow up having one person we look up too. When we're young, our role models are Goku, Superman, Barbie, Powerpuff Girls, etc. When you get old they change to Martin Luther King, William Wilberforce, etc. I have had so many people I looked up too in my twenty-five years of living, all the while missing out on the blessing of the unsung heroes that have nurtured me into this world from birth till now. Those people being my mom and dad. This poem is specifically about my pops though; a dude who didn't take the college route, but went into the Marine Corps. For a few years. Came back home with limited options, but worked his tail off at whatever avenue was open. From cleaning windows to shoveling driveways to ringing bells outside of Wal-Mart for Salvation Army during the winter. To our Westernized culture's definition of what a father should be, my dad wouldn't fit the criteria in anyway. But in my eyes, he's exactly what every father should look like. One that finds honest hustles for his family, not wanting anything for himself. One that is very slow to raise his voice in any situation. One that never complains about life's woes. And one that is honest about his feelings. Compared to any of the heroes i've ever have had, they should all take a backseat to my dad. This poem is a thanks to my dad, for being authentically who God made him to be.

"It is easier for a father to have children than for children to have a real father." - Pope John XXIII

Bell Ringer

My pops, broke as he is
Would always ask me if I needed money
No disrespect, hear me out
My dad is the kind to leave a voicemail every time he
calls
Just to tell you to call him back
The kind to stand outside Wal Mart
With bell and red donation bucket
Centered within eye of Winter
Blizzards burying boots with every blink
As watery eyes wearily winced
Nose running, frantically searching for heat
As frigid fingers shook jingles
Making sure wage's minimum maximized presents
under tree
Contentment contained if nothing remained of his gain
He's a provider
My pops showed me patience
Within the hospital of forbearance
A thunder strike could hit and burn all his clothes
While US Cellular shuts off his phone
And find himself repeating to each of his three kids
"Clean this mess on the floor"
And still not raise his voice with a volcanic eruption
He taught me to see worth in worthlessness
Whenever weary legs met accommodation of my
passenger seat
Eyes joyfully connect with cup holder as pennies sat in
there, joyfully

150

For they knew that he would happily adopt them from
my neglect
Saying in puzzlement, "how can people not see how
much your worth?"
Never ashamed to scrape up dirt to make beautiful
mountains
My dad taught me to be committed
Never one to be a passive parent
Nor bought into that "do whatever makes you happy"
rhetoric
But showed me that holiness shouldn't be holey
And outs shouldn't be options if you're in
No matter if feelings constantly debate truth
Chase what is right, not what feels right
My pops slows down my fast pace life
Like city transportation drivers that know my dad's
rugged, up point thumb well
He knew that I was always a great mile runner
But when needs go noticed, be ready to drop baton of
busyness
And go a marathon for others
He was the first one to show me that we're surrounded
by clouds of witnesses
So thunder will storm from tongues of those whose
stomachs carry dark clouds
And it will feel like their words will reign over my race
But keep pace with perseverance whether or not they
try to entangle you
My pops taught me to keep headstrong and heart soft
To never just follow a man for his authority
But by his fruit formed on fig branches
Never be afraid to sit motives down for question

Ask, out of compassion and brotherly love
Not out of faulty excitement of shaming
My pops isn't the brightest mind
But has an integrity that illuminates
He may be confused when you ask him what trail mix is
But when life goes nuts
Hey knows if he plants knees like seeds to floorboard
The sun will shine rays into darkness drying him out
My pops, broke as he is
Won't let lack attack identity
For He knows his name is held in a higher Treasury

Spitology – My Mother's King

This poem if you haven't caught it by now is about my mom. I don't want to explain too much here and in turn water down the poem. But just know, my mom is madly awesome.

"My mom is definitely my rock." - Alicia Keys

My Mother's King

She was a Topaz gem
Whose glimmer was birthed dimmer
Under dark skies where sunshine seemed nonexistent
Single parent home
Multiple home child
Who was accustomed to the breakfast of red dirt in the
morning
Words like impoverished and poor
Were no foreign terms to her
She was in a chess game
One she had no control over
Though in a position to be checkmate
She knew she would be a queen
Because her King was above all things
Above the snake infested homes
The holey socks on winter walks
Her pursuit of a better life would never stop
She could teach Drake what starting from the bottom is
Because she's here
Unwilling to let less than humble beginnings
End her in fear
Triumphant through doubts and multiple tears
Taught me that the term 'give up' would never adhere
If it wasn't for her
I wouldn't be here
For every thanks I receive
She deserves a thousand

Along with flying confetti
And live gospel music
Because that's all she listens too
This person is
My mom
First born and raised in Oakland Mississippi
Raised her firstborn in Rock Island Illinois
If you saw her in her early days
Giant spectacles
That magnified eyes of adversity
Juggling and balancing
School, work, and children
You would think she's a professional circus director
The way she never spared the rod
From this spoiled child when he got out of hand
I was sure she was once a lion tamer
Belt and spankings were revelations of God's tough love
Boldly saying
If I don't check you here
Someone out there will
My mom set the bar high as if she was building a
playground for Goliath
My young eyes would struggle to reach them
Hands trembled in awe and disbelief
That a human could accomplish such goals
My young mind
Unaware of the King that brought her through these
things
A King who found great pleasure in her
Enough pleasure to bear beatings and scars for her
Joy so pure that it colored her in snow white innocence

To her knee standing
Hand clasping conversations with her
He would be at full attention
My mother's powerful
Because she trusts in an all-powerful God
When I was a household menace
Dirty mouth like I refused to go to the dentist
Abandoned the nurture of parental care
To be caught up in the world's snare
My mom covered me in sheets of prayer
Knowing that one day I would say sweet dreams
To the nightmares that grasped my soul's caliber
Taking a blade to my old nature to cut it out
Replacing it with the King's emblem of grace
All that I am
All that I continue to be
Is because of He
And she
My mom
The mom who will persistent that my nappy hair
If not cut will deter me from finding a good woman
The one who premeditates chastisement
Towards anyone who messes with any of her babies
She's a reflection of God's love and care
So I will always dare
To thank my mom

Spitology – QWERTY

So, one day I will have to go through the uncomfortable day when I will have to apologize to my wife for this poem. Not because of anything about the poem itself, but because I dedicated it to someone who was unworthy of it. I wrote this poem when I was single, making it a goal to one day share with my wife; letting her know that before we met or even knew of each other, I wrote about her. This poem, one of the purest things I would have been able to offer her, was given to someone who trampled it. I don't say this in anger or resentment, nor do I want you to empathize for me in a way where it makes you despise this person. Let this just be a lesson from my failings; do not be so excited to deliver what's precious that you present it to the wrong doorstep.

This poem was written about the ponderings about the very thing I am using to type this explanation, and the very device that is sitting next to me that I will soon text with. The letters on a keyboard have been telling a prophetic story since the typewriter came into existence. The irony is that the very thing we text on, email with, Facebook on carry the greatest story of love and commitment, though we look high and low for such a definition. May you read this story and admire the love story of the QWERTY.

P.S. I will definitely write my wife a new poem!

QWERTY

Two vowels
There's two that have been inseparable since the
beginning
On the stepping stones of the typewriter, they met
Became closer to each other upon
the panel of the keyboard Joining in
Holy Matrimony upon touchscreens
Unrelenting to letting evolving generations break them
apart
They were meant to be together
Maybe I'm being overly philosophical as I ponder the
journey that these two letters speak
But my mind meditates on
U
Who believed that life was plain
Because 'Mr. Right' brothers who tried to pilot the life of
U took flight
So U was like Earhart
Traveling solo over a sea of tears the could oust the
Atlantic
Only seeing curves derived from flaws
But there was one who saw an amazing aviator
I
I thought U had arms that were like stone pillars in a
Roman chapel
Beautifully crafted and strong
U inspired I
Prompted palms to paint precious psalms
Poetry, pen and paper became prom partners

Pleasantly prancing upon pages, prepositions plus
pronouns
I made U a priority
A painting in an art gallery
Amongst many murals was U
One that caught the attention of I
Awakening creativity without touching physically
That would be an offense to God's imagery
When He's given I an up-close view of beauty visibly
What I is trying to say is how could I
disrespect the Artist of U's body When
there is no ring around the test tube that
sparked inward chemistry?
I was honored to have U
For I was impatient of waiting
I felt like clocks and calendars were running sprint
relays
As characters around I were winning the race towards
wedding bells
The neighbors down the block W and E weren't known
individually, but as "We"
While Jay and Kay down stairs acted silly together, but
their relationship was no joke
And I was chasing whatever was left
Only to get caught up going in circles
Round and round and round
But then I spun out on U
So I felt like IOU
All that I had
Because when God made U, He gave it all that He had
As I ponder these two keys on the keyboard
I can't help but to think about you

You are an answer from countless calls to Heaven
Asking the Father for His blessing to take His daughter
out
That fact that you are finally here is proof that Heaven
is a long travel from Earth
You and I were like blind-folded fellows playing Marco
Polo
Hands out, reaching and grabbing anything we could, to
find each other
But when we finally put our trust in the still small voice
Our hands found each other's
Where they belong
So you see when I see these letters
That sit so solemnly on the keyboard
I grow in certainty to this truth
Darling, you and I belong together
Forever.

Spitology – Be A Man

There's a rhetoric that I still to this day grow weary of. A hairy, puffed out persuasion that's seen in media, social circles, schools, and even churches: men do 'manly' stuff. I remember vividly seeing this men's retreat advertisement on Facebook, and the picture was of a power drill and other mechanic tools; welcoming the idea that these are the things that define a man. I think such rhetoric is crippling and limiting to the young boy who feels marginalized, odd, and unwelcomed with his interests that don't parallel the gender norm. This poem is one I dedicate to my son that I will have one day. I want him to read it and know that his God given destiny is his. I want him to know that he doesn't have to conform to anything the world runs too, but be true to his soul and what the Spirit leads it too. I want him to know that no matter how his journey unfolds, no matter how many mistakes he makes, no matter if he heeds my advice or not, I will love him and the person that God made him to be.

Because I can't find a quote that says a boy doesn't have to lift weights, walk with a puffed out chest, be strong all the time, and learn how to be useful in everything, let this be that message in plain language. Be you.

Be A Man

When I have a son
I won't pressure him to participate in extracurriculars
Or manipulate him to do "man stuff"
Act tough
Play rough
Get buff
Don't cry if your knees scuffed and you see blood
Though I will clean his cuts
And kiss his boo boo's if mama ain't around
I won't force a BB gun into hands and command him to
spray
Won't rip Barbie from my boy
If he and his sister play
In fear that he'll be gay
I will watch
Nerves Ignited with nostalgia
Remembering times of taking turns with little sister's
Easy Bake Oven
And how that simple play time
Paved pastures of intimacy between siblings
I won't squeeze and squash him into a stereotype or
gender role
Cause no box can cage the Lion he imitates
Nor will I tell him that live and learn is the only way
But if he learns then lives it will lead to less
heartbreaking days
And if he makes mistakes I won't shame or blame him
For I know the pain that penetrates from imperfection'
punches
I won't be a hard on my son

But if he ever moves mouth in motions of misogyny
Mumbles the "b", "h", or "s" word towards women
He'll mumble deeper groanings from belt bruises on his
bottom
Every time he bends to sit
I will teach him that girls are fine cut diamonds
That are usually shattered by thieves
Who grin while griming up their purity
Treat them different, honor their radiance
Always imagine them as paintings in fine art galleries
Stand in awe of their awesomeness
But lay not a finger on their mystery
Upsettingly or sexually
For that masterpiece was lovingly made by brilliant
artists
Whose hearts would wail if anything ever happened
One day you will find a female
Whose beauty can't be bound to picture frames
And if she is meant to be his
The Lord and her parents will grant her last to yours
I will always be in his corner
Rubbing out tension in shoulders
Whispering wisdom of ways to win in this ring
Only gained because i've once felt those pains
I will always have my son's back
And if he ever comes home from youth group with tears
in his eyes
Because the youth pastor started feelin' himself during
the "Man Up" series
To point of telling my son that he's a little girl
Best believe I am driving to brother man's home
And Lord help me not to deliver him with these hands

May I show my son battles not physically fought are
best won
When you allow your voice and heart to be the weapon
And not your hands, knife, or a gun
I will teach him his history
Not just Langston Hughes, Gil Scott, and MLK
But the Man whose image he bears this day
Not the blue eyed, blonde haired dude in every
monastery
But that debate's not worth the energy
I will teach him not to give up on Jesus
Just 'cause of the world's well-argued thesis
I will tell my son that I love him
I will command him to love others
I will tell him be okay making mistakes
But try not to make mistakes
I will tell him to do whatever it takes
To make the world a better place no matter the stakes
I will tell him remember the righteousness reflected
through his face
While remembering that others are made in the same
image by Grace
I will tell him if he likes dancing then dance
If he enjoys playing ball, then play ball
I will tell him i'll pick him up if he ever falls
And if I am not
around when that
comes to pass He
has a Father whose
love ever lasts

First World Problems

Spitology – Sallie Mae

Let me tell you something that yo parents, teachers, or motivational speaker won't tell you; college isn't the only answer to being successful. I have a handful of homies that paved their own careers and work great jobs without stepping a foot into school. Not saying that college doesn't have a purpose; just saying that purpose ain't the only purpose! Okay, that spiel is over. One goal that every college student looks to accomplishing when they are graduated is to pay off that mountain of college debt that accumulated. For years to come, they will hea from this lady named Sallie Mae. This woman is about her bank. This poem is my awkward love story about Sallie Mae, and who she is in my life...

"She take my money when I'm in need

Yeah, she's a triflin' friend indeed

Oh, she's a gold digger

Way over town that digs on me" - Jamie Foxx (Gold Digger by Kanye West)

Sallie Mae

I know this woman named Sallie Mae
We were once so close in my college dorm days
Our relationship was so one sided, you could say
She told me I was worth it
Told me I had a bright future
And she'd do whatever she needed to make that come to
pass
Paying the way
For she was so wealthy
Bought books that broadened my horizons
I was her offspring
She just wanted to see son rise
I was worth the purchase
Oh how I believed those lies
Together we conquered courses
Smashed semesters
But as I grew older in years
She started growing distant
Would make calls from a distance
With area codes so foreign
Her voice was so
Cold
Robotic
Automated
She just had too many other children to tend to than
converse with me personally
Conversations were awkward
Straight to the pockets

167

I meant straight to the point
No questions like, "How are you? Have you found a
career since we last talked?"
They were more like, "you owe x amount today, why
don't you pay now"
She'd send emails and command me not to reply, just
repay
I realized a heart-breaking truth
Sallie Mae ain't give a crap about me
There was always a third party in our two-way
relationship
College
Together they plotted as I trotted on projects
One processed distraction tactics
Pressing persuasion propaganda that said without him
would fail at life
In turn push me to pursue more knowledge
While the other would stack loans like logs over head i
a hole ridden hammock
Without yelling timber when trees tumbled over me
Burying me under debt till I no longer had breathe
Their plan was so elaborate
The expertise of Bonnie and Clyde
To this day I can't hide from their stride
Though i've tried
Changed addresses like a schizophrenic runway model
Block the number of that crazy broad
Praying that she would not bother
Even brought up this dude who was martyred
Mentioning that Jesus paid it all
So why don't you give his phone a call?

You'll probably have no other choice but to program
loan forgiveness after
Sallie Mae may be the worst thing behind Trump's
presidency
But I do have to thank her as I ponder the on-campus
days of residency
When rooms were like a Ratchet Real World episode
With seasons changing,
Channels ranging
Those close-knit friendships grew far from estranging
From collectively scrambling change
To score sausage pizza from Casey's
To long bus rides state to state
For collegiate track meets where we cheered with pride
till it was late
These memories I cherish in my heart
The teachers
Coaches
And teammates
Contributed an unknown investment in my life
Making me the man I've always wanted to be
Though still pursuing a B.A. in Psychology
I owe all my dogs for how they conditioned me
I'm indebted and in debt still
Though I feel so free when I remember what they did
for me
A wise king commended the enjoyment of life
To eat earnestly and drink wine worshipfully
For the road built of bills and emptied bank accounts is
a hard one
And such joy jogs memories around arena of nostalgia
Ponderings that no stress and anxiety can snatch

And if that emotional rollercoaster rhetoric doesn't
grab Sallie Mae's sentimental side
Making her rethink to resink that set date of next pay
Asking me if i'd rather pay tomorrow or today
I guess i'll sign up for automated withdrawal
... Gold digger

Spitology – Behind The Wire

I remember one social injustice fad that was sweeping my college campus my sophomore year; the #StopKony movement introduced by Jason Russell. It was circulated around a man named Joseph Kony; a resistance leader of a guerilla group called the Lord's Resistance Army, which was known for kidnapping young boys and turning them into soldiers that in turn became responsible for the killing of over 100,000 people. In order to positively bring attention to stop such injustice, Jason Russell produced an hour long video about what was happening in Uganda with Kony and the LRA, and what we could do here. This movement made waves on college campuses all over the United States; propelling young students that if they shared this video, and even did 'radical' things like put up posters around our US neighborhoods, it would bring the change needed to stop Kony. Spoiler alert, it didn't. The movement actually fell apart months later after Mr. Russell sleep deprived himself to a point of walking the streets bare naked. In the end, all his supporters, including I, looked like fools. With that being said, nothing has changed when it comes to promoting the wrongness of injustice solely through social media. #BlackLivesMatter, #EndItMovement are just a couple that are advocated heavily by a generation who desires to make a difference, but feels constricted to only do so by the ways of social media. It wasn't until later in my life, when I studied the ones before us who had none of these mediums to operate through but still make a greater change than any of us could ever dream of. I was personally convicted of my safety net in which I choose to make my voice heard for the voiceless. I don't say this to knock anyone who uses social media to be a voice of change, just to say that there is much more that can be done. Whenever we make that decision to step outside and help our neighbor, or create a neighborhood watch, brainstorm and execute ways to fund nonprofits that are actively fighting certain social injustices, we are making a difference and doing it in a much more vulnerable stance. When I think of great people in history that made change in the world, they ended up being killed for what they did. This was only able to happen because they placed themselves in the thick of vulnerability, not worrying about the costs in the end. To me, this is what fighting for a great cause looks like.

"Your courage draws people out of complacency into their destiny." - Bill Johnson

Behind The Wire

There was a moment when I noticed how oxymoronic
the word "realize" is
It was endorsed by a man name Jason Russell
Who prompted a sense of duty
That trailed its way into the two-way garage door of my
eyelids
Parking newfound responsibility to stop a man named
Kony
A Ugandan resistance leader
Who knew how to wax adolescent brains like charity
car washes
Rewiring refugees to bury bullets under shirts of
civilians
Though only a college sophomore
Living a 14.6 hour trip from Uganda
Jason Russell promised me
And millions of people collected around this video's
screen
That if we share this video with family and friends
Strap jaws with bandanas like bandits banding for
equality
Bodies with shirts illustrating intolerance of injustice
Righteously run rampant through our rural cities like
renegades bringing fame to his name
His infamous evil would be stopped
It was a historic day
Newsfeeds fed news like fast food
Many memes generated in congratulations

For this unfathomable event that sent invites to
everyone in the world;
When social media solved world problems
I realized how oxymoronic the word "real lies" is
Hammering, chiseling concrete delusion in minds
Making media a meager tool for social injustice
Constructed from 30 seconds of our participated time
#BlackLivesMatter made us feel like our tweets really
mattered
End It movement solemnly swore that painting red "x's
underneath knuckles
Snapping an instagram photo
While not leaving out filters would filter out the yoke of
modern day slavery
All we have to do is, sit back
Exercise fingers as they run around the keyboard
In our #FightInJustice T-Shirts with our cup of coffee
our right
Letting thought of getting up and doing something left
Somewhere in this ring, we lost the true definition of
fight
Burying narratives of black and blue bruised boxers
who lived outside the technology age
Sojourner Truth, brawled for her last name sake
Without a blog page, depicting feministic views that
were askew
But helped the hurting into carriages
Lifted women over the ditch of inequality
So they would find the best place everywhere
William Wilberforce Willingly Wrestled Without World
Wide Web
With no access to hashtags

Needing only to notice hashtags 'cross the backs of blacks
That failed to beautifully filter a photo worthy future for folks in Great Britain
And if no one would stand up in the same stance as Moses
Taking up the blood of the innocent and paint a red X through slavery
He would fight with knuckles as bare as the truth he desired to see
We all burn with the desire to do something good
To break chains like full piggy banks and make change
Injustice is dry wood waiting to be lit up
So tinder will not be sparked by swiping problems left or right
We can't talk about how wild the jungle is and be unwilling to enter it
We must face injustice to fight injustice
Leaving the one-sided mirror of MacBooks
Keyboard gangstas, Crips of compact drives, Bloods of the bluetooth era
Quit busting keys
Plant feet firmly to sidewalks
Till nerves are numb as rivals that arch anguish over Saints like Louis
Hands folded as if faith forever fused them until justice descended
With hearts that beat
Not for likes, retweets or instagram double taps
But ones thirsting for righteousness
Dried, torn, desperate to see people free

Refusing sips from surrounding faucets that
temporarily quench us
Searching for liberation that will pour out like falls
from Niagara
Extinguishing infernos of hell on Earth
That kind of justice, that kind of peace
Will cease to exist till we find the exit from our comfort
And find the
fire to fight
from behind
wires

Spitology - Ultimatums

"You have to do your own growing no matter how tall your grandfather was." — Abraham Lincoln

Ultimatums

Woe is I who is so entitled
Doing right to earn right to rewards
Secretly coveting congratulations for my devout
donations
Looking at people as profit to possess for my projects
In my mind, i'm master to the degree
That i'll accept or turn down applications of students
Dependent on how honor rolls wind into sails of this
scholar's ship
I'm the captain, and you are my crewmen
I've worked too hard to hear any different
My resume speaks for self, shouting accomplishments
from rooftop
Stacking good deeds like bricks, building my rights to
riches
My prayers are piñata poles pulverizing
The Highly-exalted priest, hoping to be rained up with
treats
I deserve the best, for I am
My talents pave the way, so pay my way persistently
At your tables, enable me to eat for free
At night, grant me the best king sized beds
And remember workers desire wages
Jesus ain't put prophets on
planet to be poor, but prosper
Win Oscars, or grouch like
Oscar when treated like trash
Green with envy, all because
no one will praise us?
Woe is I

Woe is us and our ultimatums
Wandering in a world of wants
Wanting all things that turn our heads
And if they don't come easy, we throw hard threats
If it ain't free, they'll feel the burn like sanders, building friction
Smoothing out desires to have college without charge
Maybe you're a bit more pious, fancying front seats of sanctuaries so everyone can see you
Get greeted with reverent salutations at supermarkets
Being praised at banquets for your fortitude
And if these aren't present, we can consider you absent
We're so far gone that we treat God the same
Driving teeth into the hand that feeds us bread daily
Coming to the Man with demands that contradict His plans
And if you don't get what you want, you give up
Like we have anything to offer in the first place
As if we didn't land in a sea of debt, almost drowning to death
From our attempts to trust in own credit, maxing out cards toward presents
Dumbfounded when swipes don't get accepted, so we feel neglected
By the King whose face of our reflection made the ultimate ultimatum
Take life or choose death, that's verbatim
We should be so consumed by love
That it isn't odd to hear people say "that verb ate 'em"
Woe is us
For we want the world so badly
Desire to have desires fuel our fires

Blind to brilliant blaze in bellies
That brands us with overwhelming beauty
We have all we need right this second
A great Presence persistently pursuing us
We feel it's goad grabbing us
Like a lover holding to hems of His beautiful gem
Just turn around and be embraced
And you'll find no need to pray demandingly
Make "do this or that will happen" statements
Create permanent pledges in wet pavement
'Cause His promise is concrete
Woe is I who was once so entitled
Thank God all my needs are met
I shall never want

Spitology – Snow Peas

I read a quote somewhere on, Facebook. Yes, I know. I can hear your sarcastic ridicule now.. "Facebook? Really? That's deep.." I will take those blows. But this quote really struck me with what it said: "The problem with today's youngsters is that no one peels peas at grandma's house anymore". Immediately my mind reminisced on when my parents sent me one a round trip to Grenada Mississippi for two weeks to stay with my great grandma Fon-fon and aunt Mary. This trip served for this one purpose only; to give my attitude and behavior the proper ole Mississippi check. I wasn't the most nicest kid, and was in the season of my life where I was raising hell in my parent's home. From karate chopping my younger siblings in the throat, to kicking mom in the face. I needed a serious reality check, and my relatives in Mississippi played those radical authoritarians that I needed! If I even gave my aunt any sense of back talk, I would be hostage-style tied to the world's most uncomfortable wooden chair in the middle of the sweltering, humid kitchen. For hours! I would like to say that after that trip to Mississippi, I came back a goody two shoes, but that only lasted for like a week. When I meditated those memories as I pondered this quote, I realized how blessed I was. Blessed to have people in my life invest in me, even when I was a stubborn jerk who chose to be rebellious whenever the opportunity revealed itself. Those people who invested in me; relatives, teachers, coaches, and friends, they didn't do it from a safe distance. Nor did they rely on anyone else (I mean, minus the being shipped to Mississippi like first priority mail) , but they did the hard work of lovingly disciple me into the person I am right this second. That in my case, is the most on point example of discipleship; not being afraid to have your own emotions and mental fortitude struggled against in order to show the most vulnerable, imperfect, authentic and transforming love to someone. You can't solely rely on a private school to do that, nor any church, pastor, 'enlightened' young folks, or book. You yourself are called to be the mentor in the lives of your loved ones and of those in your community who have lost hope in themselves. Learn a lesson from the old church moms, like my relatives in Grenada, and learn what it means to make a change.

"Change will not come if we wait for some other person or some other time. We are the ones we've been waiting for. We are the change that we seek." - Barack Obama

Snow Peas

Somewhere I read that
"The problem with today's youth is that no one peels
peas at grandma's house anymore"
Summers spent in Mississippi were my training
grounds
When belt to bottom could no longer make body budge
Mom would ship us to Grenada as first priority
Where we would address grandma and great as
"ma'am"
Whose bleach white hairs correlated with wisdom
Discernment that had been drawn out of discipline
When young mouths got hostile, rope would hostage
body to chair
And nose would rub with corners we were sent too
Before our descendants could make us
They'd be tasked with the hard work of breaking us
In the middle of those days our discipleship lessons
took place
With no Bible in sight, but a bowl of snow peas
Whose outer layer was thick as bamboo branches
Scratching, scarring fingers when fiddled with
Making the goal of actually breaking into one sweeter
than any heist
As green wads were freed from their safe
Eyes and hands were too busy to notice ears, and the
scripture spoken into them
As grandma riddled off proverbs and parables as we
leaned over a pair of bowls
In hand made wooden chairs, skin darkening under sun

183

In front of a house neighboring two churches in the wil(
plant withered region we were in
Though heat was hot, and work was wicked hard
Those snow peas showed me solace
Great grandma's house was a sanctuary
A place far from city's frenzies and gun fire
The holy of holies to the outer courts
A place of purpose when purposelessness pierced
pupils poignantly
I realize now what those snow peas were showing me
That family matters
The takeaway shouldn't be wait in complacency on
porch with peas
Pitifully griping 'bout how bad the youth is
Nor is it ship your knuckleheads to ma'ams
You and I are the ma'ams
When fathers don't father less, so the fatherless don't
grow up to father less
We are the ma'ams
When mothers value shorties over being called one by
dads who don't dare be deemed one
We are the ma'ams
And indoctrinating individuals with "do good" rituals
ain't the answer
Nor is dropping shortys off at pastor's house to be set
right
You and I are the church
When mothers make prayer priority for pained peep
squeaks
When fathers don't equate masculinity with moving
weight
But with humility in heart and courage in speech

We are the church
You don't need to have wisdom of the scholarly
You don't even need to have your own blood born
family, you just need to be
Speak wisdom diligently
Watch steps of community's children vigilantly
Inviting empty stomachs over for dinner
Learning their stories of survival
Love their souls to revival
My descendents in that Mississippi home did the hard
work
Praying for their labor not to return void
Trusting God's Spirit to be one I couldn't avoid
We all need that kind of discipleship
And it may call us to get off our porches and put in work
Stop complaining and start answering complaints
We all need that kind of discipleship
As whispers of His words bring bodies to humble knees
Breaking us before making us

Spitology – Congratulations, You've Made It

One of my biggest obstacles in my journey of life is to embrace humility and love for people. I believe that's the biggest struggle for all of us, whether we let our pride fix our posture or we wrestle it down daily to not enter into the God complex. I remember the event that sparked this poem well. I was at an open mic, and the featured artist was a well-known actor from Chicago. While he was performing a poem, he pointed out a man in the audience who told him that it was impossible to gain the world (speaking of riches). In short, this pissed the performer off so much that he humiliated the older gentleman publicly on stage. When we see the fruit of our long-hauled labor come to pass, and the desires of our heart stands in our grasp, we thank ourselves instead of God who provided that. In turn we view and treat ourselves like a god. Our relationships become profit. Our love for others dissipates, and our love for self is so wrapped around heart and head that it becomes harder and harder to see through a lens of humility. This poem is a reminder to me, a daily reminder that I need to hear every day of my life; What I accomplish, what I make, how many 'fans' I have will never mean a thing when i'm dead. All I can do with my accomplishments and successes achieved is point it back to a God who has my back, or else I will forever point everything back to me and have only my own back.

"Pride goeth before destruction, and a haughty spirit before a fall." - A Christian Proverb

Congratulations, You've Made It

Congratulations, you've made it
Pat yourself on the back
Raise a fist high
And punch the universe whose gravitational tendencies
Tried to hold you down
You pushed through
Those late-night grind time
Course cramming desk slamming days
Were worth it
Cap and gown
Four-year degree type
Or drop out
Who found your passion and chased it right
Early retirement is in your sight
No worries when you sleep through the night
Which makes up for the sleepless nights
Insomniac brain bombarded with brilliant ideas
Drowning out drowsiness
So you kick, swim towards sketch pad
Before dream drifts off to deep end
Growing out of reach of lifeguard ring of realization
Pulling imagination to surface of paper with poor
grammatization
Perfecting pronunciation as you backstroke in pool of
prolific ponderance
As onlookers drop jaw in amazement
As ideas that were once far overhead
Strike mind and open third eye

To your excellence
Their applaud, bathe in it
'Cause you made it
Compared colleagues whose table utensils
Illuminated with bright white privilege
Or glows emitting black power
As you moped over yours
That rusted singular silver spoon that brought bitter
taste to tongue
Every time hard times held it to lips
But you still took sips
Humble beginnings always taste like
Microwave ramen and 23 ounce arizona tea from gas
station
Reminding us our bellies that are built for buffets
Will feast at table of triumphant triumphs
And looky here, you made it
Blood, sweat, tears
Toil so intensely that your
Blood sweat tears
Literally, figuratively
Now you call shots imperatively
Your hard work speaks so encouragingly
Starting with a dream
Though bedheads slept on you
They now peer amid your scheme
Realizing it ain't a scam
They wake up now
Because you've made it
Hair done, nails done, everything did

Independent home
owner with not a
single kid? Six inch
heels have you
walking different
Newfound confidence has you talking different
You now label dudes who spit game, "lames"
Paying no attention to those you see as lower
No compassion for the unfortunate and broken
Just suggestions and slander
Maybe that's just the sign signifying success
So congratulations, you made it
Chin high as if nose bled pure excellence
Started from the bottom now you're
Well let's be honest, you had middle class privileges
But either way you ceased the day
Poop prosperity and piss perfection
Wake up every morning and praise your reflection
Success is a virus and you make known your infection
You at one time had a hispanic girl
Who others thought was pretty
But you were pretty tied up trying to just oh so be witty
Desired to make illy noise
So you did something so gritty
You let chica go so you could win 'dee city
What a pity
You took the whole dinner table
Got yours, took his, than theirs
Stomach popping out past pockets
Pride is a plate whose portions never gratifies
You were hungry, but this gluttony you partake in will
never satisfy

My friend, you gained the world
Guzzled it to gut
Stomach so big you can't see shoes
You've lost sight of sole
But congratulations, 'cause you made it right?
Jacked all trades while mastering none
Pursued ten thousand things while missing out on one
That One obvious thing above all others
Humble beginnings end when ego erupts
Withering away environment
Expanding extinction of empathy and others
You're calloused fingers no longer feel
In the process you've lost touch
Congratulations

Spitology – Daddy

When I worked as a paraprofessional for a local junior high school that I attended in my younger days, I broke rules. I can say that now since I am not employed there One night, I took two of my students to a youth group event, with the permission of their parents. During thi: long night of dealing with hyperactive, talkative teens, was asked a question by one of the students; "are you single Mr. Aubrey?" I already knew where this was going. I heard this question too many times. Because, you know, i'm like a super nappy headed stud. When I told him no, he started jumping for joy and then said, "OUR MOM IS SINGLE TOO, YOU SHOULD MARRY HER!" Yeah, awkward moment right? I don't remember what said exactly, but it pitifully parallels something along the lines of, "I'm greatly appreciative to think that you believe my personhood and characteristics are deemee worthy to be both a husband and father within your household. But I must kindly decline your invitation young one". I think it was something more like, "no, that's weird". I do though, vividly remember his response, "our mom is just lonely, and I want to see her not so lonely. That's all". The response stuck with me for the rest of the night, throughout the night, and within the wee hours of the morning. It was reminding me how one decision of selfishness can inadvertently create deep mental, emotional, and spiritual wounds within others. Single parent homes sometimes leave such scars. Whether it's a single father doing the best h can to pour out into children, and feel weak from not being poured into himself, or the single mom doing the same. The task of family was never designed to be taken care of by one, but by two. When one leaves in order to regain or keep self freedom, the family left is chained to life's hardships with one less greater support. I see the greatest definition of parental love within God. How is that? Well, let the poem tell you that.

"Two are better than one, because they have a good return for their labor: If either of them falls down, one can help the other up. But pity anyone who falls and has no one to help them up. Also, if two lie down together, they will keep warm. But how can one keep warm alone? Though one may be overpowered, two can defend themselves. A cord of three strands is not quickly broken." – Paul

Daddy

Two students once asked to me
"Mr. Aubrey, are you single?"
They didn't cheese at my corny response of
"Yeah man, like Kraft single"
But smiled as opportunities
Rang bell of right brain
Walked through unlocked doors
Sat on couch of consciousness
Dropping inspiration like pennies within cushions
As they put in two sense
"You should marry our mom"
I jokingly responded
"Nah bruh, that's weird"
As they retorted
"No, it's just that she gets lonely sometimes"
My heart became a sinking ship hitting icebergs
Realizing how cold these waters can be sometimes
When passengers
Who were in it for the long haul
Withdraw hand from helping fallen fellow
Giving jack while slowly sinking from the rose that
made their life bloom
No longer lying together to keep each other warm
Leaving one to be prevailed
As fam floats over flimsy foundation
Drifting off never to be seen again
Leaving a once three cord strand broken so easily
I thought two was better than one
I wanted to embrace these brothers
In hopes they'd emulate it to their mother
And tell them in a tone of both

Optimism and melancholy
"Daddies don't do what they used too"
I know of many single father's
Whose faces I've never seen a single time
But have caught glimpse of what they probably look like
As I see chubby cheeks of their offspring
See mothers who muster up talent to play two roles
Deserving of an award surpassing Oscars
As family photos
Look more like senior pictures
With baby sitting on lap in arms
Sporting his little backpack and lunch box
Wearing that million dollar smile
Ready to start his first day of school
And mom?
She picks up shattered remains from floorboard of her heart
Tapes, stitches them together
In order to painfully put together the best smile that Canon
Could ever capture
Before it takes shots
That she prayed would blow this nightmare to smithereens
Wake her up to that family she dreamt of
With her shorty snuggled between
Her and husband
Eyelids lifting up to take in the rising sun
Through her window like eyes
But reality rings through panes
Like boulders bust through backdoors
If it's not good for man to be alone

Why any different for distressed damsels?
What about shorties stranded on an island?
Left to grow up learning survival tactics
Clinging onto anything
Resembling a daddy during weekdays
No matter how pathetic in comparison
Something is always better than nothing
And he sees a whole lot of nothing compared to their somethings
Realizing his family anomaly in parallel to two parent homes
Hating the hole it hews in heart
Hastily seeking something to sustain that gaping wound
That can't be seen, but feel so visible
Making him feel pitiful
Searching for love in the superficial
Hoping the new shoes and clothes will comfort his soul
And the alcohol will wash away feelings of gall
And girls would gratify his loneliness whenever he'd cal
Then comes intimacy
Unexpected infancy
Relationship ending miserably
Father walks out spitefully
Mother's trust torn viciously
And another child left asking anybody
"Will you be my dad?"
I always heard two's better than one
But in hands of postmodern mathematicians
Algorithms always rearrange
Tuning heart toward vice precedence
Al Gore rhythms
Instead of aligning strings to strum

The drum of heart beat of heroic Husband
Who wrapped a wedding ring 'round world
Loving it and all her flaws
So much that He gave His life
So that his children could come home within His arms
Fatherhood is a commitment
When troubles tower downward into your universe
Breaking through thick and thin
Remember what that comet meant
How that shooting star so stunning
That seemed so distant
Decided to drop within arms
Anchoring her trust within his hold
Bear his children within her mold
We have a Father who fathers fathers
So when daddy's fail
His love prevails
For the pre-schooler, preteen, and poor parent
No greater love is more apparent that's inherent within
hearts
That a dad who's never lost has found us all
Those who are one parent down
Destined to be lost, not found
Turned from lost to found
Though we're lost, we're found
Wrapped in a robe of royalty
It is in that Man that we learn to be
Like Father, like son

Spitology – Entomology

Once upon a time I was once a work horse. Well, I still am... But just have a sense of balance now! Proof? My Freshmen year of college, at our Cross-Country banquet, the one award I received was a plaque for the "Hardest Worker". Laser precision focused, late night grind time, mission minded work is just in these veins! Which is honorable in this day and age, and is a great trait I believe! Living in that mindset all the time make you miss the beauty in living though. Waking up in the early AM and running to the computer to get to work makes you miss the beauty of the sunset, and the vibrant colors it paints the sky. Putting work above people makes you miss the beauty of loving those with the moments you've been given; your family, your friends, the strangers in your community that need to be loved and told that they matter. I have learned to slow down, to not let the world drown me in a sea of "to-do's". Heck, I still am to this day learning how. If we take time to just feel the simple beauty of breathing, to look out at that muddy, disgusting Mississippi River an be in awe of its luster, we would realize how much bigger this life is than working, grinding, and doing stuff. Just, study the ants, and compare them to the birds... And the flowers... And ask yourself, "are the ant really living more?"

"Martha, dear Martha, you're fussing far too much and getting yourself worked up over nothing. One thing onl is essential..." - Jesus

"Look at the birds, free and unfettered, not tied down to a job description, careless in the care of God. And you count far more to him than birds..." - Jesus, again

Entomology

Sparrows soar above us
As we descend down ant hills
Legs hurrying, feelers scurrying through grass
At great speeds, with great needs that weigh down
thorax
Working exoskeleton to bone
As we scale a ton of bones of other arthropods
Deceased by different sufferings, but same cause
Some dealt deadly blows by die hard diligence
Others dashed under defeat of giant troubles
Pressed down till pressure permanently pushes
posterior to pavement
We constantly carry loads of lucrative gain back to hilly
planes
Only to take flight back under skies
Sparing no time for our queen we work so hard for
Giving no attention to the King we work under
Taking chances of burning out under magnifying glass
Labor to maintain stability with all our ability
Placing weight of colony upon pincers
Unable to notice our crumbling foundation
As we toil to gain everything under sun
Only to lose glimmer
It's a habit held in these hills
And this sparrow laughs
Not at us
But for us
He tells us to consider his stride
How his wings run through winds without racing like
rats

Obtaining the early rising worm without obligation
Or checklists and coffee ringing bells in brain
He just goes with the wind
Gliding gleefully on eagle wings
Though unaware of where that next meal will arise
from
This bird says life is more than food
And worries of when, where, and why
Won't add feathers to wings
But will turn to hands
That grip, force, choke and jet eyes with mind tricks
Turning attention to lack, distract from faith
Though food is a need
for this flying breed
They wait faithfully
for Father to fill
feeder with seeds
How much more will
he provide for we?
The sparrow is a teacher to us ants
We gaze its lessons from this hectic hill of hierarchy
Maybe the answer is to not answer anxiety
Yet we still quest this question that catches us in
comparison
Like ant traps, we feed on feelings of futility
Carrying back broken images of beauty that kill colony
Envying coats that cover bees
Viewing ourselves in rain puddle reflections
Rejecting images imitated
Irritated in imperfections bore by body
Becoming abhorrent to current condition
Adding adornment to antennas to avoid self hate

Decorate thorax to enhance romanticized images imagined
Hoping the world will eat up our beauty
Like the anteater arching above us
Devouring our dignity
Making it impossible to possibly believe in our poetic persona
Our metaphorical makeup mimicking our Master's miraculous beauty
Instead we let make up cover girls
Put axe to our body
Severing self-esteem under steam of society's showering
Of what sheer beauty should look like
It's toxic in these terrains, and the lily longs to show us
Show us the stunningness in her stems
How petals cycle charmingly in the wind
These lilies make fields of land look like homecoming
Dressed better than any solo man's splendor
Dancing 'round dandelions with determined demeanor
And these flowers don't flour face with foundation
Nor do they labor over spinning threads
Living in dread of possibly looking less than perfect
They just wait for rain falls
Sit in the sunshine solemnly
Content with their beauty today
For tomorrow they are destined to decay
How much more does He
Have in store for us?
The Father, who finely fits fabrics over flowers
Will find ways to display our beauty if we didn't have so little faith in Him?

Maybe faith is that beauty we forsake
Traveling into the unknowing
Knowing he knows our needs
Maybe our hills are too heightened that
we can't even see His Kingdom What if
we've built these walls out of fear
Forgetting that we are provided for?
Worries of tomorrow swallow assurance in our Savior
Carpe diem quam minimum credula postero
Said a horse years ago
Whose words should trample our ant hill
Crumbling our concerns
Scattering schedules and plans
Flatten our flimsy fortress for family and friends
All the while not crushing us
Though part of us will die, that's okay
'Cause with us passed die hard diligence
Giant troubles that arched over our ancestors
At that death we find life
But in the deceased we learn to be still
And know God is good

Spitology – Division

They say Sunday mornings are one of America's most divisive times of day. The church folks from the non-church folks, the 'sacred' from the 'secular'. The 'saved' from the 'unsaved'. Not saying that any of this is completely the church's fault! Where it becomes strangely contradictory if we're honest, churches all over are even divide. Not just by buildings, but beliefs. The church down the street doesn't agree with the one on the corner because their members don't wear suits to Sunday service. While the other one is in deep disagreement with the 'faith statement' of the other church in the middle of town. Church is known more of how they fight within their own camps than they fight against the social issues that oppress people outside of their tents. I wrote this poem out of this realization within myself; the tendencies that I once had to be divisive of friends whose beliefs didn't match mine to the T. This poem for me was signifying of a turning point in faith that wouldn't take root fully till a year later. A turning point revealing to me that the way I put people in my box of expectations is the same way that I put God in my box of expectations; how long am I going to worship a god that I can fit in a box, as opposed to the God who doesn't live in these compartments of sacred and secular, and lives and breathes through the whole reality He's created? This poem was my introduction to start slowly removing these bricks from this wall that made my heart so divisive, to get to the True God on the other end.

"At the end of the day, we must go forward with hope and not backward by fear and division." - Jesse Jackson

Division

As a kid on up
I looked down on math
Elementary
Taught me how many oranges Tom had
After Bill took twenty
Making me question
Why Tom had so many oranges in the first place?
And why Bill
Didn't just tell Tom that he had A vitamin C deficiency?
I despised math
But one arithmetic operation surgically cut into my
young heart
Birthing a noun that would cause eyes to see section
Division
I loved division, especially long division,
I always thought of its steps as going to a neighbor's
house
Take twenty-four divided by one
One stands outside the home of twenty-four
Knocks till open door, realizing that he knew two and
four
So One would invite himself over twenty four, times
Subtracting himself from his home for twenty-four
hours
Until twenty-four had zero remainder of room in their
home
Though I made it look different
With me being the one to stand out

Willing to be firm as stiff necks, to disprove two or four, friends
Inviting them to admit my argument as one hundred times better than theirs
And if they didn't take away from my wisdom, there'd be no remainder for them in my life
From disagreements on where to play in boxes of sand
To quarrels over who's the greatest band
Even today, I feel the need to solve problems by deduction of friends brothers and sisters
Treating every confrontation conversation as a moralistic firing field for accusations
Distorted vision views very vital friends as foes
So sure of myself that I feel deeply doubted when someone's response is "no"
Knowing my exhortation isn't inevitably excellent
And disregarding discipline while ignoring instruction
Will bring destruction to the function of friendship
Accountability
Take a look around and notice eyebrows that raise like hands in agreement
For we'd all rather account abilities
Deposit resentment, while putting companions in check
Instead of saving our two cents before we go bankrupt by pride
That pushes us into the hole to the point where we search for credit to fill it
Before bars bank overhead
Omitting us from being nothing but bickering children amongst a jungle gym
The wisest man of wise men spoke of his disapproval of division

Every kingdom divided against itself will be ruined
And every household and city separated will fall
Yet we wonder why the church can't stand
When denominations are designed as denominators
Bringing each other down due to disagreements
Calling other denominations breeders of demonic
nations
From quarrels over wearing suits or skinny jeans on
Sunday
To throwing hooks on whether salvation can be kept or
took
As if fighting during fellowship will welcome those
out of place like a fellow's hip One thing I learned
about long division is that it always leaves out one
property Addition
So it will always make every effort to break things
apart, instead of build things together
Segregate instead of incorporate
Disassociate without taking time to, relate
Foolish and stupid arguments will always equal
quarrels
And negate generosity and wisdom from flowing from
our teeth
Yes, Every kingdom divided against itself will be ruined
But every empire united will triumph
You see, when I was a child, I loved division
But when I computed the Highest Solution that broke
pride down to it's simplest form
Making humility my greatest common factor
I noticed how strong we truly are when we're multiplied
They will know us by our love
So let's subtract ourselves from division

Spitology – Soma

A little Greek language 101. The word soma is the Greek word for what we know as "body". This word can be used to describe the figurative or literal usage of the word. One of my favorite theologians describe community as being a body. Community, like the human body, has many parts with different functions that are far from the same, yet they support each other. In community, everyone has a spot of contribution, no matter how minute an individual may seem. Just as the body makes usage of the foot, the eyes are made for great usage as well. If community fails to work together, community dies. When I look at how beautifully God has created this body, and how he made it a representation of how community should be, I can't help but to see every person who I encounter as valuable. They don't have to be Christian. The fact that they are living, breathing beings means they were made with a purpose and welcomed be a valuable part of this community. This is what loving our neighbor looks like to me; intimately bonding close to those we share the same space with, drawing out the best in them as they draw out the best in us.

"If one member suffers, all suffer together; if one member is honored, all rejoice together." - Paul

Soma

We reside behind blackboard of best lesson
We are that best lesson
When this body rises from rest
Plenty of parts are piecing each movement
So cohesive the way they
Never break as if bonded by adhesive
270 at birth brought to 206
Not because some bones break bonds
Or disappear at flick of wand
They just learn how stronger they stand in solidarity
One of familiarity
Team chemistry ain't a rarity
Ponder the cooperation of one simple blinking eyelid
Muscles mutually moving back and forth like arms of a
rowing team
And if one person seemed to be out of place
The whole body be laid to waste
A foot can't say that he's lame
Just 'cause he can't craft portraits so grand like the han
And a hand can't claim inability to meet demands
Only because she isn't the foot that can stand
For both bring the body to run
And if ears overheard that eyes see what lobes can't
capture
They should never disown design
For if body embodied an eye in entirety
It would watch movies silently
View lovers dancing quietly
And if ear took over in totality

It'd be blind to beauty in reality
The flowers and trees casually
Coasting through winds casual ease
God placed every part with precision, purpose and
poise
This body is one with many
And those many make one
Why haven't we learned its lesson?
Forsaken equations
Sickened to simple addition
That'd multiply mercy in man
Instead formulate hate
From subtraction and division we create
Viewing teams in terms of "us" and "them"
When them is us
Building these walls of defense
Which become the fence
In which we take offense
Pride and inadequacy
Stacked like bricks without mortar
So more tar takes hold of heart
Building calloused compassion
But let us come, pass on parables of pious peoples
Prince of Peace to Martin Luther King
Learn to live as brothers and sisters
Or perish like fools
For a kingdom divided against itself will ruin
And cities separated shall shatter
We're a body
Called to be harmony
Created with perfection in mind

Whether black, white, seeing, or blind
From such unity may hearts not resign but align
Connect arms as vertebrae of spine
Building each other up to the Head
Instead, celebrate when injustice subsides
Empathize when we hear heart cries
Grow so sick of viral attacks
That we actively sweat out sicknesses
That dare doom our demeanor
This is the body's function
When neck aches
Shoulders should suffer
If one shakes
We all should feel quakes
Take time to listen to gut
Learn lesson of body
No matter how vast the body be in diversity
Its learned to work together forever in unity
Under the same head
To the beat of one heart

Spitology – Branded

There's something I was reminded of working as a paraeducator at a junior high school.. Teenagers pride themselves so much in what they have! Think about when you were in junior high school; you begged your parents to only buy you the BEST name brand clothes so that you would win the appreciation of your peers. All the way down to your underwear, you wanted to be 'swagged out'. As a matter of fact, it didn't stop there. You studied the dialect of your peers, taking note of the cool words and terms to use, and started mimicking them! You watched countless Youtube videos in hopes to get the steps and gyrations of dance moves on point; the whip, nae-nae, lean wit it rock wit it, poole palace, pop lock, and even simple dabbing! You know that you've polished yourself in peer appreciation poise when people start inviting you to 'parties', and telling their friends and family how cool you are. In retrospect, this is obviously a mad funny and silly season of life. But you know what? For some of us, the love for the superficial doesn't change. It just looks different. When we're young adults, we hide behind our successes; our college degrees, our careers, our athletic triumphs if we pursued collegiate sports. If we feel like we don't have anything to hide behind though, we become bitter of selfs and bitter of others. People have these brandings when it comes to religion too; hiding behind how 'good' of a person they are, how much churchy stuff they participate in, how much biblical knowledge they hold under their belt, all so that people don't notice the underlying weakness. These desires to hide our weaknesses and brand ourselves by what we gain is a temporary affirmation. All things lose luster. People will only care about your great career until the next big exciting thing comes from a different direction and grabs their attention. Hiding behind things to conceal our imperfects is a long, tiring, and painful road. When we surrender to vulnerability, stripping ourselves of titles, ranks, and the superficial, we find our identity. An identity that's unseen, yet noticed by many. An identity that's quiet, yet speaks volumes to many.

"Always gon' be a bigger house somewhere.....
Always gon' be a whip that's better than the one you got
Always gon' be some clothes
That's fresher than the ones you rock....
But you ain't never gon' be happy till you love yours" - J Cole (Love Yourz)

"Don't hoard treasure down here where it gets eaten by moths and corroded by rust or—worse!—stolen by burglars. Stockpile treasure in heaven, where it's safe from moth and rust and burglars. It's obvious, isn't it? The place where your treasure is, is the place you will most want to be, and end up being." – Jesus

Branded

There's something very deceiving about shoes
The way they place urgency in mind
Checks at feet
Persuading us to "Just Do it"
Giving New Balance
Providing Keen sense
Making converts as we converse over Converse above
Jordans
Feeling as if we can defy laws of Gravity
Athletically or socially
And apparel tells lies for body as they lie on body
Crafting a false sense of protection
Reflecting a lack or abundance of style
We tie passion into shoes
Embed character into seams of clothing
But what good is it?
To decorate flawed flesh and brittle bones with
bountiful fabrics
When the most brilliant crafter
Who intelligently designed man in Genesis
Sees through us better than any X Ray
Surpassing sonograms by revealing our Spirit's deepest
cries
Our fabricated facade figuratively illustrates our
Illness
A sickness that can't be covered by clothes, culture, or
clever lingo
This virus can only be terminated
By a Physician labeled as outdated

Sin Animorphs us
Turning beauties to beasts
Shifting beast against beauty
But our animosity doesn't intimidate him
For He's a warm-hearted shepherd
Raising temp within cold blooded creatures
Transforming serpents to sheep
Shearing shame away
Yet we run astray
In hopes to stay
Within darkened, discolored coats
Fearful of being black sheep amongst peeps
But when has anything truly stood out and fit in?
These hems and seams that seem to esteem are pipe dreams
Sealing sole satisfaction within temporary fashion
But passion is fastened when we strip away rags for something everlasting
Replacing holy jeans for holy genes
And footwear for feet bare
Undisguised, revealing what's true
I'm not talking clothes and soles
But how you clothe your soul
For a glass can glimmer on the outside
Yet be stain stricken within
So a vessel can appear clean like teeth to fluoride
Yet be plaque plagued inside
Covering insecurities won't eradicate impurities
But a Lord long ago left his throne
To be stripped to bone
By whips, tails, and thorns

And hung naked in anguish
So that we could be adorned
Stamping us like the blood-stained doors of Egypt
Sealing peace within envelopes of His Love
To deliver us from evil
God desires to leave His burning love upon hearts
Like scorching iron, searing flesh when landed
Assuring us that no matter our transgressions
Our identity shall be indubitably
Branded

Spitology - Apology For Apologetics

There was a time in my life where I loved knowledge. I still love knowledge and seeking to learn new things about the world around me, but my pursuit of knowledge back then was a little different. I sought to learn about the world around me, learn how it worked, how to rationalize things, in order to be a great debater for the faith. I was ready to argue with any closed minded, animalistic atheist or individual who holds different spiritual beliefs than I; sought knowledge in order to be an unstoppable force to be reckoned with. In all honesty, my pursuit of knowledge was out of a deep fear of being wrong. I was deeply fear-stricken with a fear that always asked, "what if you're wrong about this?" In turn, I suppressed this fear by reading more books, adopt more of a linear thinking, be on the defensive when hanging out with friends who didn't necessarily believe in Jesus. I became so versed in what we call apologetics, reasoned arguments to justify my beliefs, that I started drowning out the beauty of faith. In all honesty, most people who believe in Jesus and are madly zealous won't admit that most of their passion is out of such fear as well. Many of them will read this and argue me till they're blue in the face. And that's okay. I came to a place that changed my perception of what it means to journey faith; a place that showed me that I don't have to carry so much. A place that said I can rest in the peace God gives, and not need to answer back to every blow taken against me. A place where I can let go of knowings, and hold onto an Unknowing that has been lovingly embracing me all this time. In this place, I have grown closer to God. Much closer than the collection of books, theories, and doctrines could've ever bought me. I understand what love looks like. I don't need to defend, be fearful, or apprehensive. I am loved and accepted exactly where I'm at.

"Knowledge puffs up, but love builds up." - Paul.

Apology For Apologetics

I apologize for apologetics
Those who listen, I hope you get it
There was a time when I was deeply fearful
Fearful my faith would falter
That I wouldn't be prepared
To deliver Jimmy John type answers
To everyone who asks for freaky fast reasons
For the hope that I have sandwiched into my beliefs
So adamant on shining swords for attackers
I'd replace my bible with theological theories
The "God disproves atheists" series
History, philosophy is what I'd study constantly
Waiting for the day I'd be called out in class
Or have to stand up and defend the notion that God's
not dead
To a prestigious Princeton graduate educator
Or angry Muslim dictators
Puffing out my pious pectorals
And flex self righteously
With strong rationalism inside of me
Though appearing like He man, I was closer to Wee man
Napoleon complex contaminated conscious
Believing that without head knowledge I'd stop
believing in cross
I learned to be more of a nuisance than noble
I apologize for apologetics
Those who listen, I hope you get it
There was a time we were deeply fearful
We still are
Most of us just can't admit it

That enlightenment period didn't enlighten us much
Just taught us to bury brilliant brightness
That we feared would be destroyed if touched
Science and philosophy were growing rapidly
For some reason we wanted to jack this beanstalk
And chop down these giants with religious violence
Claiming inerrancy in our ways
This is our excuse if you come with questions we can't
answer
Compete in our incompetence
Fighting to be dominant
Crosses held so obstinate
Put protest in protestant
We've become so calloused we call other Christians in
for interrogation
How funny
We argue with each other more than others
How funny
We've grown swift to damn and condemn sisters and
brothers
How did we get so far? I'm sorry
I apologize for apologetics
Those who listen, I hope you get it
Get that faith isn't forged by fear
That Jesus didn't come with core mission of
communism
Or to fashion folks with fascism
He was the exact opposite
Thank God He still loves us though we look so opposite
Please bear with me
We really ain't any different than
what you see in politics on TV Sadly

It ain't easy to accept our position as sheep among
wolves
We're weak in that world
We have control issues
Thinking if we don't say God or Jesus in every
conversation
His name will rot away in decay and His Spirit will drift
away
We've grown so obsessed with talking about Jesus
Billboard style promoting Jesus
That we forget to allow Jesus to be Jesus in us
I've learned this in such a humbling way
And it's uncomfortably comforting
Please don't misunderstand my humility
And my resilience of resisting
My doubling backing from debating isn't out of an
oblivious tongue that knows not the answers
I just know there aren't answers to make sense of every
prick and pain
But I know that a loving embrace
Putting a smile on your beautiful face
Attempt to be an embodiment of given Grace
And extending an offer to pray
Says more than a theory could ever say
We have control issues
But heck, if we're honest we all do
Forcing things to be done unto others
Than letting ourselves be done unto
Maybe we should
allow ourselves to
be done unto

Spitology – He Say, She Say

Facts: People have opinions. Everyone person in this world has an idea about what they think life is about, and most are ready to argue their case as the most right idea. This is especially true about everyone's opinion of God. Everyone has an opinion on God and who he or she is, and whether or not people will say it or not, they think that their idea trumps all others. Whether a deeply spiritual individual, or atheist individual, everyone has some loud opinion about God. In a world full of people who have voices and a bunch of stuff to say, it is hard to know what to believe. There's a story about Jesus that I reflected on as I ponder this; the day Jesus asked his disciples what people have been saying about him. Some disciples told him one thing, while others told him the other. Once Jesus heard all of this, he asked a question: "who do you say I am?" Jesus wasn't stupid, he know what people were saying about him. I believe he asked these questions to his students to reveal just what I said; everyone has an opinion. People will try to sway you with their theology about who God is or who he or she isn't, and it will drive you crazy with all the tension. In the end, I believe what Jesus was telling us today is to be true to what the Spirit is saying to your soul. God speaks through the wind that blows, through the sun the shines, through the small voice in us that says life is more than what it seems. We should not discount people completely, but realize that the greatest answer already lies within. If we're honest with our soul, and the Spirit that speaks to it, we will find God.

"Most people are other people. Their thoughts are someone else's opinions, their lives a mimicry, their passions a quotation." - Oscar Wilde

He Say, She Say

He say you're truth
She say you're a lie
He say you live
She say you die
He say you break chains
She say you're the reason there were slaves
He say you bring light to the iris
She say you're the copycat cousin of Isis
He say you're white
with blue eyes and
blonde hair She say
you're a tyrant
adamant on striking
fear He say you hate
us but at the same
time you love us?
She say you're unfair and you came here to judge us
He say you predestined a chosen few for greatness
And the rest you damn to hell in hatred
She say you're too weak to deal with darkness
That's why they walk blind by faith and face it
He say your blood shed shame from all who came
And come to trust your name, doesn't that contradict his
previous claim?
She say you push buttons
Yet in same breath says we control the game?
He say your grace gives us one more chance
So if we screw up after we'll face His wrath
She say it's intolerant to believe in one trail since
there's so many other paths

He say sinners are to be put to death
She say Christians are so unlike Christ's likeness
Hey say "repent" yet has yet to change his mind
She say "protest" like people outside religion ain't done no crimes
He say wear your Sunday's best
And women cover heads and mouths and not wear skirts
She say she should come as she is and not be shut up in church
He say intimidate, manipulate them into the Kingdom
Drag them by ankles to altar before the King come
She say if God is good as he say
Why force people to not be atheist or gay?
He say believe and don't ask questions
Shake your head and say 'amen' to the pastor's projection
She say God shouldn't be offended by interjection
And the Bible is according to one's own reflection
He say scriptures inerrant
So in air, rants and raves against all other views
She say church folks always argue, so that ain't nothin new
He say drinking will burn more than one's chest
And those who swear should be treated as a threat
She say all things in life are beautiful
And if we changed lens we wouldn't see the usual
He say arminiam or calvanistic?
She say he sees so dualistic
He say be in the world not of its digression
She say he cares not of people's poverty or political oppression

He say give your life to God, raise hands in worship, and
always pray
She say Christians have the worst control issues these
days
He say you're the definition of love
So if we know one, we can show the other
She say give respect to get it
So she it ain't receiving forget it
He say in you there's no worries or wants
She say it's normal to want to worry
He say in you there's in life
She say all she's seen in sanctuaries is death
He say we're imperfect and that's perfect
She say we always get judged by the verdict
He say compassion
She say he fascist
He say you're Son of Man
She say he shun a man
He say though theirs imposters with ball in their court
You came 'cause you the Jew wanna man
She say there's a chance she could believe again
You know of the facts and fallacies made about you
Understand that folks rather talk about you than talk
with you
Formulate theories about what you're like as opposed
to experiencing you
Some truths lie and some lies sound like they're true
You aren't intimidated by what they know or knew
In a world full of he say, she say, they say, we say
Your gentle voice in my gut asks me what I think
That's all that's ever mattered to you

Spitology - Punch Feer

This poem is one whose message has and never will cease to be relevant to me. Everyday is a fight against comfort zones and fear. A messy, arm twisting, rough and raw rumble. It's a psychological, emotional battle. I'd be a liar if I said that it wasn't hard, but it's worth it At the end of the fight, you land in greater depths of humility, love, and confidence. Right now, at this moment, even after three years of writing this poem, I am still punching 'feer' in the face.

"There is no fear in love. But perfect love drives out fear, because fear has to do with punishment. The one who fears is not made perfect in love." – John

Punch Feer

Fear
You're an eternal pester
Festering desires
 Destroying dreams
You are a pin
Penetrating my skin
And no matter how thick gets
You breakthrough it every single time
I can't stop you.
You're a bullet train
In your path my body breaks
Wakes
Up blood that runs the footpath of my tongue
Leaving an iron taste of defeat
You gripped my heart
Compelled my feet of confidence to
Stop
When my young naive intuition instilled my desire to
Allow perfect words to travel from my mind
Out through a roller coaster
Coasting through the tunnel of my trachea
Dancing through the air so elegantly
Landing upon the beautiful ears of unexpected routes
Anticipating words affirming affection
Perfect conversation
You sabotaged the line before the journey initiated.
When my heart yearned to reach my arms around
Tightly embracing the love of my life
You restrained my ligaments

Saying, "there's no way she'll be your wife"
You set bear traps that dig their teeth into the flesh of
my spirit
Disabling movement
Groaning due to deep searing pain
Your wicked chains have no limitations
You enslave everything possible
Choking aspirations that seemed probable.
You're the reason for my leaves falling out of season
Withering away as they land
Upon the wicked surface of your hand
You snatched my visiuon swifter than a thief
Blinding me from God-given abilities
So I'm living in frustrated hostilities
You seal duct tape over the mouth of my right brain
Logic and realistic outcomes govern my walk
And talk through legs and lips of left brain
You bring my brothers eyes to pain-stricken tears
My sisters shackled to shallow self images
Preventing pure minded privileges
Your persistence slowly shatters my heart
My knees dig deep into beds of soil
And sweaty palms sit over seeds
I am done.
I don't think you hear me right
I
Am
Done
With allowing 'what if' to sleep soundly upon my
thought bubble

Finished passively proving people's predictions precise
when they persist
"it's impossible to do that"
Screw that
My endorphins are expecting to explode internally
So move back
Tendons in my fingers crack and extend
Fire and pupils blend
Shock waves sent to the brain
It's time to flip tables and bring pain
I'm done with you
With being mad at myself
Cursing my health
Hiding my weakness like stealth
No more running to your lies
I'm walking in His truth
It is a seal upon my arm
A declaration for all to see
Letting you know that I float like a butterfly
Sting like a bee
Muhammad Ali
Beating till you're retreating
Done with this hamster wheel
Retired from repeating
So cheers
This is so long
A short goodbye to you
Fear
I know your name and game
that left my eyes fill with
tears. Countless nights my
heart curled up To your

voice it gave yield. Until I
realized that with God I
have a sword and a shield.
That I have a great purpose that doesn't include harm
My feet can stand firm against your swarm
I'm the pebble in my Savior's sling
He propels me forward to leave you with a sting
Bringing you to a death bed
Your trickery is unveiled to be foolish bickering
I am not afraid
You heard me correctly this time
I
Am
Not
Afraid
Wear my hat backwards and sag my pants a little
Because I lost fear of judgement
Go to McDonald's and purchase two Mcdoubles
Because I lost fear of the scale
Delete ChristianMingle that guarantees a single
Because I lost fear of not knowing
The one who God yokes me with for old growing
I've Unlearned the laws of gravity
Free falling into the sky
The impossible is possible and probable
Your barrier was hard to climb
But I now bound over like an obstacle
My skin is too thick
Your tricks won't penetrate
My dreams are His promise
It's impossible to stop them

Fear
You used to be the pain in my side
The excuses I made when I failed
But i'm not blind anymore
I'm done reading messages in braille
Give me a pen or a pencil
Spell your name with two e's
Because I lost my fear of editorial error
A glimmer of light pierced through your dark clouds of terror
No longer do I see failure when I look in the mirror
I see a Man
Whose path is secured
Vision unblurred
Sickness is cured
Fear
Used to be called the class jester
But unfortunately I am expelled this semester
I punched Feer in the face

Spitology – Thy Will

After my first engagement ending from unfaithfulness, started to realize something when it came to me and relationships; I never had any luck with them. Only being in four relationships ever, they all ended with both parties getting hurt. Whenever one relationship ended, I would frantically scurry to online social dating mediums, punch in my preference of a perfect mate, and scroll through countless pages of single women, who were scrolling through countless pages of single men. It sounds kind of shallow when explained that way, but here's the thing I learned after my last heartbreak; we all desire to write our own romance novels for our lives. I mean, it only makes sense right? It's our life, so we should be able to do whatever we want with it. In a culture saturated with chick flicks, Disney movies, How I met Your Mother and The Office, it's easy to get sucked into this urge to go out with the intention of finding someone who will want you. Whether that means being on Tinder for countless hours, surfing the friend's on Facebook to 'reconnect' with; we end up believing if we're not on the prowl, we are behind and will be deemed losers by our peers. Then when we find that person who's available, we cling unto him (or her) with all we can. Skipping the friendship phase, rush through dating in order to find that 'happily ever after' in the wedding. This is how we think it goes, but most of the time it doesn't. We end up being physically, mentally, emotionally abused by someone who at once seemed so perfect. After a while that relationship ends, and we are back at square one, once again on the prowl to find someone who will love and accept us. We call it perseverance, but I see it as a lack of patience and honesty to self. What I found out after my first engagement was that I sucked at writing my own proverbial romance novel. It never finished through, was full of run-on sentences, erase marks, tossed out chapters, and writer's block. When in control, I find myself in situations that drove me out of control. The truth is, if we are to have a life of true adventure, risk, and that 'happily ever after' as they call it, we have to be willing to retire our position of a storywriter, and give that to God who's been crafting stories from the get go. Whether you believe in that worldview or not, hopefully we can agree that some things that stay in your control end up falling to pieces. Outside of our control, life is full of uncomfortable mystery. Never knowing what is going to happen the next second, day, or hour. But in and of that, we learn to be okay with that, and know that a great story is being crafted by a Greater being. It may take years, it may take decades. Heck, it may just take a day or a month to find that person to journey through our chapters with. That becomes least of our concern though, for we fall in love with the Storywriter and the novel He allows us to be a part of.

"Life is either a great adventure or nothing." - Helen Keller

Thy Will

I've burned the bridge to a broken city
Made sure to record their narrative in notebook
So I could share their stories with strangers
Heck, I've lost desire to ink these tales
Finally figuring out these feeble fingers
Were never as good as an author as audience assumed
These hands once held so holy
I praised their persistence
How they gripped granite and girder
Grinding tirelessly to construct tall tale towers
Edited and embroidered with elegant emeralds
Whose glimmer reflected from streets of gold
Pathway paragraphs paved with passion
Sweat stains still shining in solid cinders
That swerve and sway
Through hills and highways
To a castle standing so colossus
Crafted
Curved to complete perfection
With crystal white walls that towered
Over all other creation in kingdom
I idolized my illustrations
Believing I painted perfected pictures
With poise and prolific glory
Though writer's block bested me
Cutting off road to creativity
After many late night brain storm sessions
Wee hours of cramped carpal tunnel

From typing lengthy pages of text
Curious to what's next in my own novel
Only for it all to crash and burn
Slash and burn
Damaged, burnt from salvaging scorched scripts
Only to have ashes slipping slowly through fingers
Knees dug in aftermath of failed equations
Formulas thought to have no fault
Finding myself returning to dusty drawing boards
Revising theorems thought to be perfect
Good will hunting made the search seem so easy
But i've truly learned how mopped up I am
Pen and pad in hand proves
How vulnerable to abuse
I really am
With words I thought I was a wizard
Oz outwitted this fellow
Every time I attempted to open the door or thee
(dorothy) Cyclones of curiosity swept these feet from
foundation
The Wicked witch of west would wreck my writtens
With witchcraft that decomposed courage
In this lion heart
Turning me to a tin man
So cold i'd scare crows
All I wanted was someone
To make this heartbeat feel like it's there
But obviously I had no brain
If only I trusted yellow brick road before me
I'd find after
An artisan whose written way before me

Whose more than a big head in heaven
Staring down at those bold enough
To ask for anything
But came from behind divine drapes
To be one man cast for curtain call
To call curtains to fall from front of us
To see a greater Author
A romance Novelist
Burning with desire to
Revise
Edit
Rewrite every love story
But requires our pen and pad to do so
Submit all work to His desk
Desire to be a character
And hand Him the task of editor
This is no easy task to ask
For we all aspire to be wordsmiths
Shaping sagas ourselves
For only we know our lives
And what we desire to be in it
But we must admit
The constant heart breaks that make earth shake
Wiping tears that tower down over ink
Smearing, smudging sheets
Making illustrations illegible
Tearing out pages after unseen plot twists
Is ripping hope from our hands
Leaving paper cuts that kill joy
We were never made to be authors
Build cities and skyscrapers

Only to see them in shambles
But this Author wrote world to existence
Splash spirit like water colors
Over leaves to change with season
Used pastels to paint
Picture perfect portraits
That have a way to know what to say to souls
The sunset the kisses the forehead of ocean
How gentle winds woo snowflakes
Sweeping them off their feet
How fall leaves descend into
Welcoming arms of earth
Love stories have been His forte
He asks us to trust him in its adventure
So I burn down bridge to broken city
One that should've never been
But in the end I find a beautiful start
Swap sayings for unsaids
Absolutes for an abyss
Security for open planes and a blindfold
By faith following footsteps
Without feeling around
Embarking on journey
Where there will be wars to fight
Battle scars to secure
Demons to beat
And a beauty to sweep off feet
I've gave the pen and pad to God
Trusting this Author will write
The best narrative any man or woman
Has ever read

Spitology – Elegant Enigma

I remember when I was a player (yes, there was a time in my life where I was 'suitable' looking enough to hav the opposite sex at least acknowledge me at the very least), there was always something that quickly frustrated me about girls.. And that was how they keep everything so darn secret! I mean, fellas, empathize with a young brotha real quick! Whenever you text girls, they are NEVER quick to respond. And when they do, we get a "hey" or a "hi" back... Or how about when we're really wanting to take a girl out to the movies, or homecoming, but we want to know that they think the same about us... But they NEVER give any cues to a mutual interest in us. That stuff used to to make me do two things; either give up and look for some other girl who'd give me all the answers and affirmation I desire or just be 'straight up' (advice to young guns reading this.. Never ever be 'straight up'...). 'Straight up' sounded something like this: "yo girl, I like you. When are we gonna go and make out?". It was the perceived leap of faith into a shark tank with dynamite that was ready to go off the second we hit water. Nine years late from 'dem heathen days', I still see that frustration wit people my age; "why doesn't she give me any indicator that she's interested in me? I mean we always talk, han out, etc. But she keeps everything to herself!" What I have learned personally is that this trait girls and women have are probably a reflection of what God is like; a God who loves to be pursued. The journey that women are, like God, is one that calls for our full attention. If I find someone who deeply catches my sou and eyes, I know that there will be a journey to understand and get to know this person. That impatient side of me will bark down my ear canal saying "she ain't worth all this toiling and venturing bro, give up!" or "Just be 'straight up' bruh. Tell her you tryin' to throw a ring on that!" That's just the battle that presents itself in this journey. When I think about it in this way, I think about how dope God is, as well as that trait that women have. This poem may come off as an encouragement to girls and women, and if its received that way, dope! It's more of a reminder to me to never give up an easy traveled path, but remain a narrow road (I know some homies is hating hard on me for saying this..). In that place, I have no choice but to be in great wonder and awe; being forced to mature. In this place, I remember how God is worth journeying and pursuing. How a relationship is far from religion; I don't have to make myself look good, or 'woo' God for the benefits. But know that all He ever wants is my uninterrupted attention. That part of Him will never die, and we should never let it die in women.

Elegant Enigma

She shed tears that tore chasms in my core
Sat down upset in tension that turned tummy
Bore fears that smears smile to stationary state of
suffering
And this shook my soul severely
So I sought solutions to soothe psyche
So I asked, "What's the problem? How can I fix it?"
In a choked up, frustrated, agitated tone she told me
"The only problem to fix is your perspective"
If i've been convinced of one thing
It's that God has granted His greatest quality to queens
An element evident in phrase "false evidence"
How no mention of good can go without evil being
prevalent
And how rugged ribs of Adam shepherd something
stunning and feminine
Though it brings puzzlement
We experience great wonderment
That women, like God
Can't be fully figured out
Both beings elegant enigmas enveloped in eclectic
energy
A pricey narrow path pilgrimage
Demanding dudes to drop coins and cash before
commencement
Bury bag and belongings before beginning
Sacrifice shirt, sandals, shoes, and walking staff before
start

And trust in trail where toes embark
Eve's emulators entail us to enter an enduring
expedition
Accumulate all authentic attention
Her road isn't a race for runners
Replicating rabbit's rapid reckless routines but
Suiting slow tolerant tortoise who take time
With no intentions to sprint or cut course
But embark every tall hill and long valley
Skyscraper and dark alley
Play no games, no dilly dally
Knowing struggle signifies a grand finale
But in a generation of instant ramen and fast food
We favor cheap and quick fix
Get digits, get with it
And chill in Netflix
Search Tinder for a few
Find a chick to try to woo
And if she won't go for you
Dude cops attitude like
"You're stuck up, stingy
Acting priceless but ain't worth buck fifty"
We're broke, so deep in the hole
We lost sight of how to invest
Blew profit and burned checks
Trash credit, so indebted
But we forget it
Settle for small inch over great miles
Trade chivalry for misogyny
Turning mystery to misery

But it makes sense looking at history who repeats
himself
We have a tendency to place God on same shelf
Making "us" time so minimal
Spending little time or none at all
Only in need we give a call
Besides that, the relationships one sided
And we don't mind it
'Cause we know we're loved no matter our involvement
You
God who reflects woman
Woman who reflects God
You are worth our attention
Worth the journey that doesn't have an ending point
Even when walking exhaust our joints
You're a blindfolded pitfall
With winds whisping past or bodies at brilliant speeds
Your drop has no bottom to reach
But every second ceases a moment to teach
For you're a lesson whose wisdom has no empty class
on Earth
Woman, young girl
Don't emasculate nor domesticate your divine design
Always remain that mystery to men like me
Don't call us after receiving our numbers
Texts us only after two years, and only with a simple
"hey"
When we inquire of your name, tell us it's "a mystery"
And married maidens
Never ever, no matter how much it gets on our nerves
Never tell us what's wrong when we wonder

But remind us that a simple embrace
A word of affirmation is the only necessitation that'll
bring alleviation
Remind us, that like God
You are worth our attention
That you just aren't the journey
But the passenger by our side
Not to be taken advantage of
But to experience the
beauty that's discovered by
our eyes

Spitology – Little Light

I was literally just driving home from a meeting when I randomly started thinking about this old Sunday school song called "This Little Light of Mine". It's also worth noting that this song was considered an anthem during the Civil Rights Movement. Anyway, I was singing this song in my head, and just thinking of it's implications today. How this light that the song speaks of, can be easily burned out or misused by humans. In a country that lives values realism, logic, facts, knowledge, which are all very good things, the deep spiritual things get despised and cursed. Proof of this could be how the art is something that's less prevalent within the school system. Art, which is creative, out of the box thinking that leads people ultimately to consider life outside of the things seen is no longer important to the growth of a human being in America, according to our school systems. Cold, robotic thinking is our creed, and is attempting to blow out every flame that works against it. Like I said, nothing is bad about knowledge; this is coming from a person who loves studying history, psychology, and philosophy. I love having conversation with people about these disciplines. If we are completely honest with our inner man though, our souls hunger for something that books smarts can't satiate. When we look at nature and how the sky looks when painted by the sun's rising and setting, there's something in us that experiences life. When we watch movies of passionate love, something is us says "that is beautiful, and I can't fully explain why". When we ignore the spiritual in the world, we are grieving something within us that's good; something that desire to show us great beauty, great hope, great peace, and the greatest Love ever experienced. This poem was a reminder to me to never let this world distract me from the beauty that God is. Never let myself be so distracted by a world full of thoughts, opinions, biases, and facts, that I lose sight of something I have experienced first hand. Something that has transformed my personhood. Something that burns within me. Never let that light diminish.

" You're here to be light, bringing out the God-colors in the world. God is not a secret to be kept..." - Jesus

"I hear an almost inaudible but pervasive discontent with the price we pay for our current materialism. And I hear a fluttering of hope that there might be more to life than bread and circuses."

Little Light

Preacher man told her she had a little light
That the biggest star
Touched down and died to become her rising sun
And His lumosity illuminates through little children like her
Such truth brought beauty to beam from brows below and chin above
Causing eyes to act as lamps leading light through limbs
Making her appearance radiate with rays
Brightness that burned shadow's deathly valleys violently
Waking up courage from subconscious slumber
This little girl was like New York City atop darkened mounts in midnight gloom
A dwelling that inhabitants couldn't help but notice
Like flies to ultraviolet lights
Trapped by attraction
To something their souls knew would burn away burdens
People
Pious and impious
Purged to purity in her presence
She was a torch in the hands of a Champion
With fire filling her every fiber
Though physicality wasn't a reality for Him in this age
She felt His Spirit soar her soul like somber seas
Hovering healing over cracked and torn foundations
Building every broken building back up by new blueprint in red ink
He was a fire billowing smoke into stratosphere

Signaling how her trespasses had been burned and
blew away
Her little light shined so unapologetically wherever she
went
Every word she spoke
Every deed she did was a product of her little light
But older she got
The easier it was to suppress
Wherever there is light
Shadows follow close from behind
With intentions to rule over radiance
Some living in silhouettes would snicker
Deeming her a child with head in clouds
Telling her that little light was insufficient to bringing
sight
Her daydreaming disgusted them
Other shady seemingly smart fellows would tell her the
moon made more sense
That believing in the sun disdained doctrine of logic
The sun and moon can't both exist in same atmosphere
You're either hot with irrationality
Or stone cold in truth of reality
And to them she was sweating
Others would come with severe sun bruises
From fellow sun bearers who played with fire
And brimstone that broke broken beings to more
brokenness
Souls sadly seared by sunlight they were told would
give them fight
They were angry
Aiming misdirected wrath like large bricks at her
window like heart

Saying "if your sun is so good, why do I have these burn marks?"
"Why would your sun let darkness exist?"
She was circled by those condemning the combustion in her core
Indoctrinating her with their materialism
Proselytizing her with their religion
Snatching hope from her hands like a child ripped from fingers of a mother
She started to forget what preacher man told her
Found it more comforting to be a basket case
Pail placed over that little light
Though emissions of its exuberance exited blaze into bones
Keeping its shine to self seemed like the only painful option
Keeping shine from self was the plan she adopted
Raising skepticism in her disposition
So she dissed positions she was placed in
Trapped in office of low pay towards self esteem
Hourly waging war in cubicles of self condemnation
No benefits or options to retire
Just full time torment
Though she disowned his throne
Sun didn't cease to adorn her torn scorn demeanor
His light could never be put out
Always first to her fallen stature when life's alert rang
Faithful when she was faithless
Graceful though she thought He was graceless
Preacher man said to that little girl long ago
In this world you will have trouble
Hurting human beings will hate your joy

Persecute your personhood
Question your fortitude
With attitudes and intelligence
And poetic magnetics that pull you from apologetics
But stand firm
Because that light has overcome the world
Even when it feels frigid in foundation
And salvation seems so simple minded
Search that silent voice in secret place
Seducing you to "seek"
And you will find that little light shine
Was never designed to make sense
Or be condensed by cathedrals
But to comfort like arms warmly embracing us from evil
True love never makes sense
But when you're in it and it resides in you
You care not whether it's false or true

Spitology – Dreams

Well, they say save the best for last. This poem was the first one I had ever performed.

The poem that started this journey that led to this book that you have in your hands. As I sit here writing this, I remember how I believed my dream to be a writer would just remain a dream. I thought it would die to the realism that was preached by people who gave up on their dreams. I hate being that cliché person by saying this, but never give up on what your gut tells you that you are created to be. Whatever passion burns within you, trust that though it won't be an easy road, and that it will come to pass with a step of faith out into the unknown. Or heck, maybe it won't but the journey toward it was the goal itself. There's nothing unique about what I do, at all. I write poems just like everyone else. The only thing that makes the difference is a stage half the time. What I would want to encourage and inspire people through what I do is that the only thing that was profound about it was the step of risk that I took, and continue to take. No matter how dim the light gets, or how cold seasons grow, I answer to the challenge. Dare to dream, and not only that, but fearfully follow that dream. The world will always give you reasons not to, and distractions will always try to entice you. Trust that the God who created you and your novel will make one heck of a story through the trials.

"I just can't give up now
I've come too far from where
I started from
Nobody told me
The road would be easy
And I don't believe He's brought me this far
To leave me" - Mary Mary (Can't Give Up Now)

Dreams

Today, a child asked me this question
When you were my age mister, what was your dream?
Though this question held innocent simplistic curiosity
The hand of my mind's philosophical complexities
Drew a gentle, tangible finger to my lips
Ceasing the tongue to draw out words of sense
And instead would dribble from my lips were
utterances of
"Uh
Hmm
I, oh"
I didn't know
Though the question was far simpler than Pythagorean
theorem
Or the formula to configure serum osmolality
My mind drew nothing
A blank canvas of unsolved reality
In this moment of solid uncertainty
I gave permission to myself
To dunk my cranium into the
Apple bobbing barrel of buried aspirations
To find my motivation
And provide a sober, fulfilling answer
For this child and myself
My mind jump sped to infinity and beyond
The humble beginnings of the toys and stories
That brought great nostalgia to my heart and soul
But beared no fruit for my psyche's empty bowl
Like a touchy break
I abruptly stopped

To the days when I was a Washington Warrior
A school that bled red and black
That greatly symbolized my
Externally dark skin
And internally fiery zeal and passion
That lit flames underneath my feet
That never failed to incinerate the numerous
Laps of the
Four hundred meter ovular footpath
Fused with polyurethane and cement
Where young, fervent competitors with
Great hubris stepped up
Only to depart in great shame
To my absolute tactic of game
Oh I was young, gritty, and reckless
Shooting for the top place of great history
Looking to leave a legacy
Paved by a figurative bloodbath of flawless victory
That's it
That's where I first encountered my dream
I was gassed up with childlike conceit and self-esteem
I dearly wanted and yearned to be the fastest man alive
But couldn't foresee the storms
that i'd have to dance through
To boldly say that this dream
was derived But where did it
die?
Was it when I was in the school of high?
When I raised my white flag to those who said my
dreams wouldn't fly?
Making girls, drunkenness, and friends the center of my
life?

I was blind to my dying dream
Suffering multiple wounds of a knife
In my youth
I birthed life into my dream
And the world slowly eradicated its glow and gleam
But it seems that this dream remembered that little
Brown eyed boy
That created it with great childlike enthusiasm
And refused to yield to this brown eyed unrecognizable
beast
That was going through destruction
Solemnly swearing that it would hold on for that brown
eyed boy
Even if it meant falling martyr to a devilish decapitation
That's it
That's the answer in bold print
My dream passed away early
It, he, died with honor
And I was too stuck in my ways to care
I continued to run
And I ran, and I ran, and I ran
And I was running off the single power that was slowly
faltering
Like the eiffel tower
How could hell succeed in making me so sour?
But hold on jack
Rise back to your feet and fix your crown back
Though the seemingly dark end to the story
Seem like a great end
There's a chapter of great radiance
That casts out the darkness

That beckoned for your soul
Just like it did your dream
It happened when I was at the year mark of twenty
I fell to my knees and wept
For my sunshine life started to fade
And no more did it feel like sunshine
I was all alone
No friend to phone
My dream dead and gone
I finally came to the stark realization that
I was traveling the wide path of the wrong
And in the midst of it
How I wished I could've remembered the lyrics of this
song
I just can't give up now
I've come to far from where i've started from
Nobody told me the road would be easy
But I don't believe He's brought me this far
To leave me

Unfin-

.... We are unfinished fragments.

Made in the USA
Las Vegas, NV
21 February 2023

67910882R00144